The Colonial Background of the American Revolution

The Colonial Background
of the
American Revolution

Four Essays in American Colonial History
By Charles M. Andrews

New Haven and London: Yale University Press

Copyright 1924, 1931 by Yale University Press
Copyright © renewed 1958
Revised edition, September 1931
Twenty-third printing, 1975.

Printed in the United States of America by
The Colonial Press, Inc., Clinton, Massachusetts.
All rights reserved. This book may not be
reproduced, in whole or in part, in any form
(except by reviewers for the public press)
without written permission from the publisher.
Library of Congress catalog card number: 31–24004
ISBN: 0–300–00268–8 (cloth), 0–300–00004–9 (paper)

Published in Great Britain, Europe, and Africa by
Yale University Press, Ltd., London.
Distributed in Latin America by Kaiman & Polon,
Inc., New York City; in Australasia by Book & Film
Services, Artarmon, N.S.W., Australia;
in Japan by John Weatherhill, Inc., Tokyo.

To my Wife

With Appreciation and Gratitude

CONTENTS

Foreword

CHARLES McLEAN ANDREWS was one of the most distinguished members of a group of American historians in the first third of this century who pioneered a new interpretation of the colonial period and the American Revolution. Most earlier writers had regarded the English colonies primarily as embryonic states of a future American nation. After narrating the events of the years of settlement, they had emphasized chiefly those developments in which they saw the beginnings of a distinctly American society with its own particular virtues. The mother country played little part in their accounts except as an unwelcome source of outside interference with strictly American communities. When that interference became intolerable, the Revolution followed. The new group of historians adopted a very different approach.

Andrews and his colleagues held that the way to understand the colonial period was to study these colonies primarily in terms of what they actually were for a century and a half before they became independent states— that is, as political and commercial dependencies of England and integral parts of her far-flung territorial and economic domain. It was necessary, he believed, to examine the relationships existing between colonies and mother country, the slowly emerging British system of colonial control, and the theories, economic as well as political, upon which they were based. A study of the

Foreword

development of colonial society in all its aspects was also important, not so much for the sequel in the nineteenth and twentieth centuries, but to help one understand how these transplanted Englishmen and their descendants gradually evolved patterns of life and outlook so different from those of the mother country, and why they became restless and dissatisfied with their condition of colonial dependency.

The historian or his reader, so Andrews believed, must stand, as it were, on the shores of England and look across the ocean at the American colonies, and at the same time be able to place his feet in the Western Hemisphere and look back at the British Isles. Such a feat of mental gymnastics would give a sort of double-exposure view by which alone the historically minded American of the twentieth century could gain an appreciation of the actual nature of the colonial world; only thus could he understand, first, why the British overseas experiment was for long so extraordinarily successful, and then, why it failed so spectacularly in the second half of the eighteenth century. The origins of the American Revolution were to be found not merely in the events of the dozen or so years just before the Declaration of Independence, but in the history of the whole colonial period on both sides of the Atlantic.

Among Andrews' many books and articles on colonial history, none stated this point of view more effectively and clearly than the series of four connected essays which he called *The Colonial Background of the American Revolution*. Nowhere is there to be found in relatively short compass an analysis of this subject at once so penetrating and so readable. First published in 1924, the book was

Foreword

ostensibly addressed to his "fellow workers in the field of American history"; in reality it was written for all those readers who cared enough about the beginnings of this nation to put aside their prejudices and preconceptions and listen to what a careful scholar could tell them as the result of a lifetime's study. He wrote the book during that decade after the First World War when it was not always easy to persuade Americans to look at their early history objectively and without passion. It was a time of reaction against the crusading zeal to make the world safe for democracy which had characterized the war years, a period of disillusionment with the ways of the Old World powers with whom we had been in temporary alliance and of contentment with our own attitudes and habits, an era of narrow nationalism in politics and diplomacy and— what concerned Andrews most directly—in the writing and teaching of American history. Some of the distress he felt about the attitudes of many of his fellow citizens is reflected in these pages.

Yet this book is anything but a mere tract for the times in which it was written, soon outdated, and valueless for a later generation. On the contrary, it has an enduring quality that makes it important reading for historically minded Americans in the 1960s as well as for those of the 1920s. During the years that have passed since Andrews wrote we have gone through far more difficult times, at home and abroad, than had the first readers of this book, and we have attained a broader view of this nation's place in the world at large, a deepened sense of national responsibility, and a greater awareness of the importance, for ourselves and for the whole world, of the American experience. Now more than ever should Americans benefit

Foreword

from an understanding of that national experience. Now more than ever should they profit from the studies of America's leading historians. Now as never before should they, as Andrews wrote in the closing words of this book, "exhibit honesty, charity, openmindedness, and a free and growing intelligence toward the past that has made them what they are."

Leonard W. Labaree

Yale University
March 1961

I.
The British Colonies
in America

The British Colonies in America

MORE than three hundred years ago a small group of able-bodied men landed on the soil of Virginia and founded the first permanent English settlement in the New World. This famous plantation, though numbering in its earlier years but a few hundred souls and for a decade a victim of sickness, starvation, and a faulty system of government, was always more than a setting for the romantic adventures of John Smith, John Rolfe, and Pocahontas, more even than the birthplace in America of self-government and the cradle of a new republic. It was the beginning of a great experiment in the field of English colonization and overseas expansion, the starting point of a great world movement which to-day has spread to the farthermost parts of the earth. Our own country, which is a product of this movement, emerged from it as an independent national state, but only after one hundred and seventy-five years of membership in the British colonial family; and it is in the light of such association, therefore, that the colonial period of our history must be approached and, in the first instance, judged.

The planting of a settlement in Virginia was a commercial enterprise, undertaken by certain private individuals for the purpose of enlarging the trade of the English kingdom and of bringing a profit both to themselves and to those who had invested money with them. These English promoters were authorized and encouraged by the crown, and their work was carried on during a period when England was engaged in intense naval activity and was making daring raids into the lands and waters where her arch-enemy Spain was in control. The enthusiasm that inspired this group of Englishmen sprang from the colonizing experiments of Portugal and Spain; from the stirring tales of England's own navigators and their semi-piratical attempts to break the Spanish monopoly of the West; and from the implicit faith, widespread at the beginning of the seventeenth century, in the boundless wealth and resources of the lands, still largely unexplored, which, like a world of mystery, stretched toward the western horizon.

The colonizing movement, once begun, grew with great rapidity, and during three-quarters of a century (1607-1682), for various reasons intimately bound up with England's own history, men and women crossed the Atlantic and found places of permanent abode on western island and mainland. Thus before the end of the seventeenth century the sphere of English occupation in the New World encompassed more than twenty settlements, which extended from New England to Barbadoes. Whatever may have been the antecedents or the motives of these early colonists who defied the dangers of sea and wilderness and established the first English frontier in America, the fact remains that in the process of adjusting themselves to their new environment in temperate, semi-tropical, or tropical zones, they presented marked peculiarities and wide contrasts in modes of settlement, forms of agriculture, and conditions of social life. Furthermore, as they added to their numbers by birth or accretion and extended their interests by land in search of homes and in search of markets by sea, they exhibited ever more clearly marked group distinctions and variations, which now we recognize as those belonging peculiarly to New England or the Middle Colonies or the South or the West Indies, as the case may be. The reactions of these groups to conditions both in England and in the colonies themselves produced what we now call the colonial history of our country.

At the beginning of the seventeenth century no precedent existed for so novel an adventure in the field of maritime endeavor as that in Virginia promised to be. England, it is true, had a few palatinates along the Welsh and Scottish frontiers, a few plantations just begun in Ireland, a group of incorporated merchants residing in the Low Countries across the Channel, and here and there a trading factory in India; but her own history furnished her with no successful example of a permanent settlement three thousand miles away from her own shores, and the experiences of other nations gave no clue to the proper treatment of such a settlement or to the place it should occupy in any system of colonial administration. In other words, England began her career as the greatest and most prosperous colonizing power that the world has ever known without any fixed policy, in fact, without any clear idea of what she and her people were doing. When for one reason or another and for ends of their own devising, these Englishmen were leaving their country and going to lands far distant and little known, their government was giving scarcely more than legal sanction to a migration for which it was in no way responsible.

Thus the planting of these communities in America was

not the work of kings or men in office, nor was it promoted according to any carefully planned scheme of conquest or with any desire for territorial aggrandizement. With the exception of Jamaica, New York, and Nova Scotia, each of which England seized by force—one from the Spaniards (1655), the second from the Dutch (1664), and the third from the French (1710)—all these settlements were founded by private individuals or groups of private individuals for certain specific purposes of their own. Some of these people wanted religious and political independence; others aimed at commercial profit; many fleeing from the hard conditions of life in the old countries, sought land and a living for themselves and their families in the wide spaces of the New World; while a small number, in somewhat the spirit of the old vikings, were stimulated to action by the salt of pure adventure and the glamour of the sea. All crossed the water, sometimes with royal sanction and sometimes without; and their settlements grew into communities of frontier folk, which in large part were beyond the range of royal interference and royal control. In reality these settlements were not colonies; they were private estates, the proprietors of which, both corporate and feudal, were endowed with wide powers and privileges, conferred upon them by royal charters. There were the feudal seignories of New York, the Carolinas, and the Bahamas, whose owners had an eye to profits from trade and the rent of their lands; the similar seignories of Maryland and Pennsylvania, where a religious refuge and a holy experiment were brought into being under the legal protection of feudal lordships; and the separatist communities of New England, whose founders established religious Puritan commonwealths in the wilderness, and wanted to be let alone by the authorities in England that they might worship God and fight the Devil in their own way.

Even had the English government been able to conceive of a colonial organization at this period of its history, it would have been unable to develop a workable policy as long as it allowed these settlements in America to remain under private control and to manage their own governments and own their own soil under the terms of the charters granted them by the king. Certainly the early Stuarts never tried to fashion a colonial policy, and their successors after the Restoration were hardly more aware than they had been that a colonial world was in the making. It is true that, more or less unconsciously, both the earlier and the later Stuarts were laying the foundations of a system that became very elaborate as the years passed; but at first their purposes, which were commercial rather than political or administrative, were based on the idea that the communities in America were agricultural plantations or tenancies rather than colonies; that they were valuable less as political organizations and centres of population than as farming areas, outposts of trade, and sources of wealth; and that they were to be monopolized on the productive side wholly by the mother country in accordance with the prevailing idea that the maritime kingdoms of Europe should keep their plantation trade to themselves. England applied this idea first to the tobacco trade of Virginia and Bermuda—almost the only trade of importance which she had with her American plantations before 1660—and required that the planters should raise such staples for export as England wanted, should avoid all trading relations with England's Continental rivals, and should ship their surplus products only to English ports. In return for these restrictions upon their commercial freedom, England granted them a monopoly of her own market, forbade the raising of tobacco by her own people at home, and placed heavy duties upon that product from Spain and other foreign lands.

This policy of monopolizing the trade of dependent colonies was effectively applied before 1624 in the tobacco contracts with Virginia and Bermuda, but after 1628 it could not become operative on a large scale because England was distracted by dissensions at home, and without command of the sea was unable to carry on her colonial trade with any degree of success. Certain private promoters —the Warwicks, father and son; Sir William Courteen and Ralph Merrifield, merchants of London; the Reskeimers, Delbridges, and other adventurers of the southwest; and certain private companies organized for trade, of which there were many with interlocking memberships—all these engaged in a lucrative traffic in various parts of the world. The English government as such not only had no part in their enterprises, but probably held some of the promoters under suspicion as opposing the prerogatives of the crown and encouraging parliamentary ideas. In fact, until 1660 England's relations with the colonies were only fitful and sporadic. In 1624 the king annulled the charter of the Virginia Company of London; in 1635-1637 he attempted, with the aid of the Laudian party and under pressure from Gorges, Mason, and Morton, to overthrow the Massachusetts Bay Company; and in 1652 the government of the Commonwealth reduced to subjection the colonies that were royalist in sympathy, Virginia, Maryland, Barbadoes, and Bermuda. But these activities were no part of a common plan; they were merely the expression overseas of political and religious differences prevalent at home at this time. But after 1660 and the restoration of the Stuarts, a colonial idea emerges for the first time in English history; and the commission, which was sent to America in 1664 to capture New Netherland from the Dutch, received special instructions—namely, to investigate conditions in New England—which have a true colonial ring. But this commission failed of its purpose; and as affairs at home improved very slowly, official supervision of the colonies remained in a very rudimentary state. Even the famous navigation acts of the years from 1651 to 1696 were at the bottom commercial not colonial, and England's interest in America during these years continued to be a matter of trade and not of organized control. Englishmen were feeling their way, as it were, passing laws and appointing councils for the oversight of trade and plantations, merely in the hope of making these distant agricultural settlements profitable to the mother state. At best, however, the efforts of this period were disordered and ill-directed, and the attempts that were made to put into efficient execution the regulations laid down in the various acts of trade and navigation make these years a time of almost hopeless confusion in methods of colonial management.

But with the rise of France under Louis XIV, Englishmen gradually awoke to the inadequacy of their own efforts and the failure of their own methods; and from

Background of the Revolution

King Charles down they began to feel admiration when they saw the great French minister Colbert (1661-1683) inaugurating a well-conceived plan for the founding of French colonies and the advancement of trade, and building up across the Channel a powerful commercial machine. Charles II, always fascinated with the French principles of government and easily drawn within the circle of the Bourbon influence, agreed with Louis that the Dutch were dangerous competitors and should be destroyed. Others, though not agreeing with the king that the Dutch were greater rivals than were the French themselves, saw in the French system a model for their own, and argued for greater unity and centralization in government. De Foe in 1704 advised Harley to become "an all-powerful prime minister of the type of Richelieu, Mazarin, and Colbert," that he might check the "confusion of councils" which prevailed in England and prevent the "errors in executing and unwariness in directing" due to the number and inefficiency of English ministers in office. English merchants viewed with envy the establishment in France of a highly centralized system of boards and councils for the prosecution of commercial enterprise, and called the French Council of Commerce of 1700, which was designed, they said, to regulate trade without fettering it, "a piece of clockwork, which by its springs directs the wheels in their motion." In England men of the day were despondent because of the apparent breaking down of the old standards and the general loosening of the ties of society and religion. Evelyn wrote to Pepys in 1701 that never had the nation been "so atheistical, false and unsteady, covetous, ungrateful, lewd and luxurious, self-interested, impudently detracting and uncharitable," as at the time when he was writing, and he feared that "without a miraculous and undeserved providence" there would be "a total dissolution of the government and constitution."

Furthermore, Englishmen soon began to realize that this growing French monarchy, under an absolute and aggressive king, was neither a dying Spain nor a mercantile-minded Holland, but a rival young and vigorous, one to be respected and feared in both Eastern and Western worlds. They saw themselves threatened by a power whose commercial ambitions were very much like their own. They watched with growing uneasiness the movements of the French in Canada, along the Mississippi, and in the West Indies, as well as in the Levant, India, and Africa. They began to be alarmed, lest by losing their trade on land and their commerce and fisheries at sea, they should be shorn of resources already recognized as the necessary buttresses of a wealthy and growing state and they could but contrast the apparent efficiency of a centralized dominion, such as that of French Canada, supported by a body of intelligent and warlike seigneurs possessed of energy and leadership, with their own small, scattered colonies, each absorbed in its own affairs, inclined to peace, and resentful of outside interference even on the part of the crown to which they were legally subject. Consciously these Englishmen were condemning their own system and admiring the better-disciplined economy of the French; unconsciously and almost in spite of themselves they were following, as always, the ideals and instincts of their race, based on individual initiative and responsibility, qualities destined to make them a great nation of colonizers and commonwealth builders.

Background of the Revolution

Men rarely envisage the trend of their own time, and these English mercantilists could not foresee, as we see to-day, that the policy of Louis was to lead eventually to the economic ruin of the French nation, whereas their own seemingly chaotic system was to usher in an era of almost unprecedented economic prosperity.

Thus it is not surprising that British statesmen in their concern for the security of trade and the necessity of adequate military defense, should have thought it wise to bring these loosely controlled and privately managed colonies into a closer unity under the crown; or that later, when the demands of trade and the pressure of the French peril in America actually made a solution of the problem imperative, they should decide to transform all the colonies into royal provinces and to administer them directly by means of royal officials and more or less after a common plan. The idea seems to have originated with the members of the Lords of Trade—a committee of the Privy Council, specially appointed in 1675 and entrusted with the supervision of plantation affairs. In 1678 they were influential in bringing New Hampshire under the crown. In 1681 they succeeded in modifying, in some very important particulars, the terms of the private charter which King Charles had granted, quite against their will, to William Penn. In 1682 they enunciated a definite policy by denying the petition of Lord Doncaster for a grant in Florida, and by announcing that it was not convenient for the king "to constitute any new propriety in America, nor to grant any further powers that might render the plantations less dependent on the crown." The next year they refused a charter to the Plymouth colony on the ground that whenever the king gave away his right of government, he found it almost impossible to enforce the acts of trade. Convinced, as they said, that it was of very great and growing prejudice to his Majesty's affairs in the plantations and his customs there that such independent governments be kept up and maintained without a nearer and more immediate dependence on his Majesty, they urged the king to consider the plan—never lost sight of by those opposed to the Puritan theocracy of Massachusetts—of consolidating a group of colonies under a single head appointed by the crown. The king and the Privy Council accepted the recommendation of the committee, and taking advantage of the annulment of the charter of Massachusetts by process of law in 1684 and the conversion of the private propriety of New York into a royal province, when James II ascended the throne in 1685, they created the Dominion of New England, thereby transforming all the territory from the Kennebec to the Delaware into a single crown colony.

Undoubtedly the model for the English Dominion of New England was the French Dominion of Canada, but the act of consolidation itself sprang from the necessity of enforcing the laws of trade, and of preventing the French seigneurs from advancing farther into the Indian hunting grounds of northern New York and encroaching on the frontiers of Maine and New Hampshire. The experiment might have withstood successfully even the bitter opposition of the reactionary Puritan leaders and the tactless administration of Andros had not the king at the same time deprived Massachusetts of the privilege of having a representative assembly which that colony, as well as most of the other colonies, had enjoyed for half a century. Furthermore, though the dominion was overthrown by the revolution in Massachusetts in 1689, it might have proved successful under William III, had he been interested in the colonies and willing to uphold the Lords of Trade in their policy of bringing the plantations into direct dependence on the crown, but he was too busy with more pressing business to give much thought to the situation in America. The separate governments were allowed to return to their former condition; Massachusetts under her new charter of 1691 became a semi-royal colony; and the "dominion" idea of colonial government was abandoned.

Now with France as her greatest competitor, England became engaged in a titanic struggle for supremacy at sea, that is, in the world of commerce. Colonies meant trade, trade meant wealth, and wealth meant power, and power was the ultimate end to be gained in a conflict among maritime nations, where trade and conquest went together, and where, according to the doctrines of the time, competition, not coöperation, was the watchword. As the men of the eighteenth century saw it, this commercial rivalry was a mortal combat, to which the colonies were expected to contribute their part in furthering the victory of the mother country. Thus under William and Mary, Anne, and the first two Georges, the English government strove to make the colonies contribute to the advancement of England in the European world. It was inconceivable that they should be allowed a commercial freedom that would be all to the advantage of the enemy; while to suffer them to remain weak and disunited, with the French on their very borders, was to endanger the resources upon which England depended—fish, furs, and naval stores—and might easily result to England in the very loss of the colonies themselves.

Nor was the English government alone in this view of the case, for there were colonists whose opinion is well expressed by Captain John Nelson, a Boston merchant of wide experience, who had taken part in the overthrow of Andros, had served in the militia, and had suffered as a prisoner of war in France. Writing to Secretary Shrewsbury in 1706 or 1707 (the paper is undated) he says: "The principal and greatest defect and mistake we have hitherto lain under is the number and independency the one from the other of so many small governments; whereby our strength is not only divided and weakened, but by reason of their several interests they are become and do in a manner esteem each as foreigners the one unto the other, so that, whatever mischief does happen in one part, the rest remain unconcerned. By this disunion our strength is weakened, whereas, were the colonies of New England, Hamshire, Plimouth, Road Island, Conecticutt, New York, etc. joined in one, we should then be at least 15 for one with those of the French in Canada, and might reasonably propose that, instead of a bare defence, we might be in a capacity, with the assistance of some ships from England, to make an entire conquest upon that place." Whatever may be the colonial policy of Great Britain to-day, certainly *laissez faire* was not a doctrine that played any part in determining England's relations with her colonies during our colonial period. Nor was there anything in the conditions of that time, from the nationalistic point of view, to warrant England in adopting a "let alone" policy toward the colonists in America. On the contrary, everything in the situation confronting her demonstrated the utter folly of such a course. Under the pressure of this conviction, in the period from 1696 to 1754—a period of American colonial history shamefully neglected by the historians— the statesmen and merchants of England formulated for the first time a clearly defined and widely accepted theory of colonial relationship, now familiar to us as the old British colonial system.

In order to execute the regulations already laid down in the navigation acts, King William commissioned a new Board of Trade and Plantations in 1696, and in the same year parliament passed a new navigation act, extending and strengthening acts already in operation and providing for their better enforcement. The Treasury enlarged the customs service in the colonies, which had been called into existence for the collection of the "plantation duty" imposed by the act of 1673; and issued to the collectors and others, through the commissioners of customs, new instructions for the performance of their trust. The Admiralty created eleven vice-admiralty courts up and down the mainland and in the West Indies, largely for the purpose of checking illicit trade and aiding the work of the customs officials. The Privy Council and the new Board of Trade sent mandatory orders to the governors in all the colonies to bestir themselves in whatever concerned trade and navigation, to take oaths and give bonds, and to assist by every means in their power officials sent over from England for the purpose of furthering the new policy. The secretary of state for the southern department was instructed by the crown to specialize in colonial business and to take upon himself, as no secretary of state had ever been called upon to do before, responsibility for the colonies, chiefly along administrative and military lines. Finally, parliament began to enlarge its own sphere of legislation by passing an occasional act which affected the colonies as well as the rest of the British world in other respects than those of trade and commerce. Thus was begun a movement toward uniformity of control and centralization of management notably in all the royal colonies, but also, to some extent, in those that were still in proprietary and corporate hands.

However, no movement of this kind could be successful as long as any considerable number of colonies remained apart under private authority. The new board moved slowly. Two months after its first meeting, realizing that the colonies could not be united again under a single governor (for, as we have seen, the "dominion" idea had been abandoned), it recommended that all be placed under a common military head or captain-general, who should have the powers of governor in any royal province as long as he remained there. The next year it came out strongly against the revival of any old or dormant claims to lands in America, on the ground that to revive such dormant titles, after the decision had been reached not to create any more private colonies, would lead to unspeakable disturbance and confusion. Then, in 1698, having become more familiar with the situation overseas, it decided to adopt the policy which its predecessor, the Lords of Trade, had recommended when, in a representation of 1689, the latter had informed the king that if "the said proprietary and chartered governments do not speedily comply with what is required of them, we see no means to prevent the con-

tinuance of this mischief without calling in the further assistance of parliament."

This threat to call in the aid of parliament was ominous
and portended trouble. The private colonies were certain
to resent any encroachment upon the powers granted to
them in their charters and to construe any interference by
the crown as an infringement upon their liberties. The fact
that some of the colonies had been in private hands for
more than half a century and had established traditions
and habits of self-government that were deep-seated in
the lives of their people and the practices of their governments, made England's task a difficult one. To take away,
after so long a period of immunity, the privileges that the
crown had already conferred and under the protection of
which the private colonies had grown to strength, was sure
to rouse vehement protest and lead to charges of illegality
and oppression. Massachusetts had already demonstrated
these facts. On the other hand, were England to allow
these privately managed colonies, the weakest links in the
chain, to go their own way, she might find herself thwarted
in any successful application of the new principle of control, already laid down, and thereby suffer great losses in
her contest with France. According to the accepted theory
of colonial relationship, the colonies were the king's and
that which he had given he could take away. The situation
was a delicate one, calling for the utmost discretion and
good judgment on the part of those who were entrusted
with the oversight of colonial affairs.

The most troublesome period was bound to be the first
ten years after 1696, which, unfortunately for both England and the colonies, coincided in part with the War of

the Spanish Succession. England was trying to render more efficient the whole customs service in America and to bring about a more orderly execution of the acts of trade. She was calling on the colonies to adapt their commerce to the restraints imposed by the navigation acts and was setting up vice-admiralty courts, in which the English customs officials in the colonies might prosecute offenders against these acts. She was sending over agents with roving commissions to inquire into conditions and to report to the authorities at home the success or failure of the new methods of royal control. No wonder the air was full of charges and countercharges, bitterness and animosity. Royal officials of the kind demanded for the prosecution of this business had rarely been sent to America before and were thoroughly disliked, as would have been any functionaries despatched from England to investigate colonial affairs. No sooner was the new system installed and in working order than complaints began to come in from the crown's agents to the effect that the proprietary and corporate governments—the Bahamas, the Carolinas, Pennsylvania, the Jerseys, Connecticut, and Rhode Island—were evading the navigation acts, harboring pirates, refusing to submit to the authority of the new officials, and obstructing the new appointees in the performance of their duties. Exaggerated and even false as many of these charges were, some of them—particularly in the case of Pennsylvania, the Carolinas, and the Bahamas—were true enough to convince the executive authorities at home that if the colonies were to be of any use to the mother country, the process of unification would have to be continued until all the private proprieties were brought into a closer dependence on the crown. In 1697 Secretary Shrewsbury issued a solemn warning, threatening the governors of the royal colonies with the loss of their places and the proprietors and corporations of the private colonies with the loss of their charters, if they did not "guard better against breaches of the acts of trade."

But as time went on and conditions in the private colonies did not improve, the Board of Trade renewed its threat to solicit the aid of parliament. Convinced that the "humour" prevailing in these proprieties and "the independency they thirst after" had become so notorious as to call for immediate action, it recommended that the charters of these colonies, "intitling them to absolute government," be resumed by the crown, "without prejudice to any man's particular property and freehold"; and it declared that such an act of resumption could not be accomplished more effectively than "by the legislative power of this kingdom." Consequently, in 1701 it made an attempt to push through parliament a bill providing that the chartered colonies, that is, all the private colonies, be reunited to the crown. But this bill failed to pass, as did also a second bill prepared by the secretary of state in 1706, and amended by the Board of Trade, granting the queen and her successors sole power and authority to govern the private colonies and to appoint their officials, "the said power and authority [so runs the bill] to be forever united to the imperial crown of this realm." Another measure, formulated in 1715 and designed to regulate the charters in such a way as to render the private colonies more amenable to the royal will, never advanced beyond the preliminary stage. Though the House of Lords seemed to be willing "to bring the colonies to a better sense of their duty," the colonies resisted the measure by every means in their power and the growing Whig element in the House of Commons was opposed to any tampering with vested rights.

Despite frequent changes in the personnel of the board, each new group of members, without regard to its political affiliations, maintained the traditions of the plantation office. In 1719, in a report to the Lords Justices, the board restated its policy and declared "that all occasions should be laid hold on to recover the dominion [if not the soil] of all the proprietary colonies into the hands of the crown." Its one attempt after that date to interest parliament in the matter, made in the year 1721, failed because the members of the cabinet could not agree to present the recommendation to parliament as a governmental measure; and also because the proprietary and landowning class, which considered the rights of landed property and other private franchises more important than the interests of trade and commerce, controlled the House of Commons as well as the House of Lords, and thus was able persistently to thwart any policy advocated by the Board of Trade.

Convinced at last that a general plan for royalizing the colonies with the aid of parliament could not succeed, the Board of Trade modified its recommendation, and urged parliament to pass a bill increasing the authority of the crown over the private colonies in America and making more effective the enforcement of the prerogative there. Three times was such a recommendation under consideration—in 1734, in 1744, and in 1748—having in view "the better enforcing of his Majesty's orders and instructions throughout the plantations." But instantly the colonial agents sounded the alarm against this extension of the power of the crown, of which, as Robert Charles, agent of New York, wrote, "but few within [the] doors [of parliament] or without were at first apprised," and succeeded in warding off the threatened danger. Thus, once more, constitutional issues in England saved the private colonies, and parliament, despite the efforts of the executive authorities—represented by Horatio Walpole, auditor-general of the plantation revenues, Francis Fane, standing counsel to the Board of Trade, and the Board of Trade itself—refused to do anything whatever to strengthen in America that prerogative of the crown which it was gradually reducing to a minimum at home. Unwittingly, it was making ready for the day, twenty years later, when Hillsborough could object to a New York petition, as "drawing into question the supreme authority of parliament to bind the colonies in all cases whatsoever," an assertion which, in the opinion of William Smith, Jr., the historian, privately expressed in 1769, "would one day have serious consequences to both countries." Before 1750, when parliament wished to prevent any increase in the royal authority, it protected the chartered rights in America, but after 1763, when it determined to uphold its own authority, it refused to recognize any claims that the colonists were making on behalf of their liberties. Parliament would not permit either king on one side or colonist on the other to impair in any particular the sovereign powers that it was gradually and self-consciously acquiring for itself.

When after 1706 it seemed likely that parliament would not assist in sweeping away the proprieties at a single blow, the crown, acting through the Privy Council and the Board of Trade, revived earlier expedients in order to make the king's prerogative effective in America. In times of "extraordinary exigency" it was accustomed to claim and exercise, under legal advice, the right of appointing a provisional governor over a proprietary colony, even though the charter had not been surrendered—as it had done in Pennsylvania (1692-1694) and Maryland (1690-1715) and was to do in South Carolina (1719-1729) and in the Bahamas (1718-1734)—but this was only a temporary expedient preliminary to a return of the province to the proprietor or to a final surrender. But now the board, blocked by parliament, recommended that the crown deal separately with the proprietors and secure the entire annulment of the charters "either by purchase, agreement, or otherwise," thus reverting to the method already employed in the case of Bermuda, Massachusetts, and the Jerseys. The crown had deprived Bermuda and Massachusetts of their charters by process of law in 1684, had made the latter colony partly royal by the new charter issued to her in 1691, and in 1702 had persuaded the proprietors of the Jerseys, whose claims had always been doubtful, to surrender their rights of government without compensation.

But the new ventures of this kind were only partly successful. Negotiations between Penn and the Board of Trade, which had been going on since 1703, came to a sudden end in 1714, owing to the fall of Harley and the Tory ministry and to the death of Queen Anne, and proposals by the heirs, after Penn's death, even on to 1727, came to nothing. Connecticut and Rhode Island refused in 1723 to surrender their charters voluntarily. Two attempts which were made to vacate the Carolina charter by law failed because estopped by the privilege of peers, and it was not until 1729 that the proprietors, with the single exception of Lord Granville, who retained his eighth part of the proprietary revenues of the province, finally surrendered, at a price, both soil and government. The charter granted to the Georgia trustees in 1732 provided that Georgia should revert to the crown twenty-one years later; and in 1717, after a struggle lasting more than a decade, the government of the Bahamas was wrested, also at a price, from the hands of those who represented the original proprietors of forty-seven years before, though the ownership of the soil was not obtained until 1734 and final title not until 1787 when it was vested in the crown by vote of parliament.

Thus it happened that by the middle of the eighteenth century every British colony, except Maryland, Pennsylvania, Connecticut, and Rhode Island, was in the king's hands; and even in the proprietary colonies of Maryland and Pennsylvania, which were returned to their owners in 1694 and 1715, traces of the royal connection remained. The deputy governors, who were appointed by the proprietors, had to be confirmed by the crown; the Penns lost the power of vetoing the laws passed in their colony; the governor of Maryland could not leave the province without the royal consent, and the laws enacted by its assembly, having been subject to the royal approval for twenty-five years, were expected to be sent to England for the king's inspection, a requirement rarely, if ever, complied with.

The corporate colonies of Connecticut and Rhode Island were under attack in one form or another half a dozen times between 1720 and 1770, and it is not always easy to understand why they, too, did not lose their charters. After 1723, when they refused to surrender their charters voluntarily, various suggestions were made to force them into line with the other colonies: namely, to convert them into royal colonies by depriving them of their charters; to change them into colonies of the Massachusetts type, by issuing explanatory charters; to join them together as a single crown colony; or, by adding them to New York or New Hampshire, to destroy their identity. But not one of these suggestions was acted on, and, to the end, Connecticut and Rhode Island remained private, self-governing colonies, beyond the immediate governance of the crown. All the colonies acquired by the treaty of 1763—Canada, the Floridas, and the Ceded Islands in the West Indies— became crown colonies at once, although, as it happened, they did not receive representative assemblies until some time after the cession.

Thus of some thirty or more colonies possessed by Great Britain during our colonial period, all but four eventually came directly under the control of the king and were governed according to a common plan. Largely because of the opposition of parliament, the executive authorities in England never succeeded in royalizing all the colonies and so laying the foundations for a uniform and centralized system of colonial administration; but they did succeed in royalizing most of them and in setting up a plan of control that was practically the same in all cases. After 1763 Great Britain, victor in the contest with France, was the head of a group of dependent communities stretching from the Gulf of St. Lawrence to the farthermost limits of the southern West Indies. Each was administered by a governor, a council, patent officials, and provincial officials, who by solemn oath swore allegiance to the king and looked to him as the legal source of all their authority. The very possession of such a colonial world transformed Great Britain from an island kingdom, such as she had been in Elizabeth's reign, into an oceanic dominion, and broadened the scope of her responsibilities from the four seas of the seventeenth century to the ocean-wide activities of the eighteenth. She became the centre of a far-flung line of settlements, which acknowledged the king as their sovereign, herself as their mother country, and her institutions as models of their own; and as far as the colonists thought about the matter at all, they accepted their connection with her as the normal condition of their lives and essential to their welfare and prosperity.

The only bond that held these British colonies together was their legal subordination to the authority of the British crown, for owing to various causes, such as isolation, local environment, religious differences, and admixture of racial stocks, they lacked the unity that might have been theirs had similar religious, economic, and social practices been common to them all. Yet, always, though more or less unconsciously, they tended toward uniformity of governmental procedure and used similar methods of increasing their self-governing powers. From 1690 to 1711 and again from 1744 to 1754, commissioners representing New England and New York and sometimes other colonies met at Albany or elsewhere for the purpose of taking the offensive against the French or of establishing more friendly relations with the Six Nations. Also, considerable coöperative intercolonial activity was stimulated by the various wars in which the colonists were engaged; but only when the British government took the initiative—and rarely even then —were system and efficiency, on any large scale, attained. They looked on each other as "foreigners," in the mediæval sense of the word, that is, as men of other communities, and frequently used the term to designate their neighbors. It is true that from time to time during the colonial period they evidenced some slight manifestations of mutual understanding, but except for Franklin's plan of union—the Albany plan of 1754—which met with little favor among themselves, they took no concerted action that can be interpreted as a self-conscious desire for union among themselves.

Undoubtedly, many of the colonists, as groups or individuals, favored some sort of combination under a single military or political head. Governor Hopkins of Rhode Island wrote in 1755, "The present situation of affairs in North America may show how little dependence can be had, even in times of greatest necessity, on voluntary union and quotas of men and expenses, and might serve to convince some who seem to love and understand liberty better than public good and affairs of state how necessary a solid union of all his Majesty's Northern colonies is, and how vain that expectation is which supposes the same good ends may be attained by any partial one or by such an one as every colony may make or break just as they please." But, generally speaking, the colonists were opposed to any federal scheme that involved a sacrifice of local power or autonomy; and to the end of the period the colonies remained a group of separatistic, individualistic communities, subject under the law of the British constitution to the king's will and pleasure. Only the two proprietary and the two corporate colonies lay outside the king's immediate control.

Thus the leading features of British history during our colonial period can be summed up in the words "expansion" and "centralization," processes which manifested themselves in ever widening spheres of commerce, colonies, and ocean supremacy. Britain's policy in regard to her plantations was to secure a more closely knit and efficient colonial administration in the interest of the trade of her merchants and the receipts of her own exchequer; whereas the colonials, though they accepted their obligations as loyal subjects of the crown, early began to strive for greater freedom of action than that which they had as colonies in the strictly legal sense of the term. As they found it increasingly irksome to meet the obligations imposed upon them by the customs system and the courts of vice-admiralty, they broke the law by which technically they were restrained, and trenched upon the prerogative to which legally they were subject.

During the troubled years from 1701 to 1713, England was carrying the double burden of waging a war with France and Spain and of setting in motion her new machinery of colonial control in the face of considerable colonial opposition. The struggle between centralization and local self-management, between the power of the prerogative and the practices of the popular assemblies, manifested itself first in Puritan New England, where segregated religious communities, believing passionately in their own systems of religious belief, government, and social order, resisted, even to the point of revolution, the attempt of the mother country, employing the agency of the Andros administration, to

draw them within the confines of its own commercial system. Soon the trouble spread to the proprietary colonies
and gave rise to the complaints from Randolph, Quary,
Basse, Mein, Bridger, Larkin, and other English officials
of the crown in America. These various and numerous complaints and the answers they called forth show the determined opposition of the colonists at this time to any seeming encroachment on their chartered rights; and make clear
that whereas they justified themselves in trespassing with
impunity upon the accepted constitutional powers of the
crown, they would not allow that the king had any business
to interfere with their rights under the charters, even when
there was considerable doubt as to what those rights were.

After 1713, when the war ended, the friction between
the crown and the colonies grew less, partly because of the
decline of piracy and the cessation of charges of illegal
trading with Scotland, after the union of that country with
England in 1707; partly because after 1706 the English
government stopped sending over special agents and obtained its information through the governors and other
regular officials in America; and partly because the colonists had begun to find the new conditions less exacting
than they had feared. But generally speaking, the friction
was never absent, because few of the colonials rose above
the petty affairs of everyday life and government or looked
beyond the borders of their own particular colonies into the
world beyond the seas. That they never understood, or
sympathized with, what England was trying to do or construed her policy otherwise than as it immediately affected
themselves, is not surprising, for their interests did not
coincide with those of Great Britain and they could not be

expected to sacrifice their home concerns for the sake of promoting the material advantages of a people so far away. As they did not make such sacrifices for each other, why should they do so for Great Britain? A few prominent men —Bellomont, Dudley, Dinwiddie, Shirley, and Pownall, for example—took a larger view of the situation, and seemed to grasp the mercantilist idea that colonies should be useful to the land of their origin. They seemed to understand also that England was engaged in a life-and-death commercial struggle with France and that the fate of the colonies was in some way inevitably bound up with that of the mother country. There were others, too, particularly among the merchants and planters, who realized that the connection with England was essential for their own security and prosperity. But by far the greater number of those who sat in colonial assemblies or were influential in shaping colonial policies scarcely gave a thought to the problems that were burdening the minds of the statesmen at home. They not only did nothing to aid in the solution of those problems, except when to do so coincided with their own interests, as in matters of military defense, but always opposed any plan that seemed to benefit the mother country without compensation to themselves. The reasons for this attitude are readily understood when one considers the second great feature of colonial history, the growth of colonial self-government.

No colonies hitherto established by any power in any part of the world had been permitted to govern themselves, though the municipal autonomy of Spanish America came nearer to it than anything else. We cannot say that the instinct for self-government is something inherent in the members of the Anglo-Saxon race or that the privilege of self-government is one that should be exercised as of right by any body of Englishmen that happens to voyage beyond the seas for purposes of trade or colonization. Self-government was not promised by the vaguely expressed rights, privileges, and franchises mentioned in some of the early charters, nor can it be traced to the practice of parliamentary government in England, which in the seventeenth century concerned but remotely the mass of the English people, and furnished neither precedent nor example for the government of a colony. During the years of our colonial history, there were instances in which representative self-government was not enjoyed, as in Virginia before 1619, in Salem before the arrival of the Massachusetts Bay Company, in Barbadoes before 1639, in the Puritan settlement on Old Providence island, 1630-1641, in New York before 1691, in New England under Dudley and Andros, in the Bahamas before 1729, in Georgia under the trustees, in Nova Scotia before 1758, and in Canada from 1763 to 1791.

Legally, a colony was always considered an inferior and subordinate corporate body, similar in type to the gilds, boroughs, and trading companies of England, all of which exercised self-governing powers but within certain defined limits. In the past such powers had been granted to boroughs and companies by the king in royal charters, on the principle that local affairs, to be well managed, should be self-administered, and that inferior corporations, in order to preserve local law and order, should have the power to make the rules which they were to enforce. For two centuries many of these lesser corporations in

Background of the Revolution

England had, up to a certain point, managed their own affairs; and as early as 1407 an interesting precedent was established for corporations residing out of England, when a group of English merchants, living and doing business in the Low Countries, was empowered by the crown to govern itself. Though the powers that a trading company might exercise had hardly become fixed at this period of the seventeenth century, nevertheless by 1606, when the Virginia companies of London and Plymouth were created, the practice of self-government was the rule with trading and other corporations, and was conferred, though not in all essentials, upon the two Virginia companies in that year.

These companies, it will be remembered, were not colonies but the promoters of colonies, and remained in England, whence they despatched the ships, men, "tackle, apparell, municons, and furniture fit and necessary" for the founding of colonies. The Virginia Company of London established the Jamestown settlement in Virginia, and after twelve years of experimentation with autocratic and monopolistic rule, finally granted to its colony the same privilege that it itself enjoyed, under its charter of 1612—that of gathering the "generality" into an assembly for the making of wholesome laws and ordinances pertaining to the safety and welfare of the colony. The popular assembly thus authorized in Virginia, unlike the "great and general quarter court" of a trading company, took a representative form, because the character of the scattered settlements rendered a gathering of all the free inhabitants difficult and well-nigh impossible, and demanded the adoption of a usage borrowed from the parliamentary system of England, namely, that of sending deputies to rep-

resent the local "towns, hundreds, and plantations," each
of which was erected into a borough for the purpose. Who
the voters were or how the elections were conducted, we
do not know. That all the "inhabitants" took part is impossible, for there were many servants in the colony who
could have had no part whatever in the voting.

The granting of the right of self-government to the
settlement on the James is justly regarded as of great significance in the history of America. Of equal significance
is the fact that the grant was not revoked in 1624 after the
fall of the company and the taking over of the colony by
the crown. When in that year, for the first time in English
history, the king and his ministers found themselves with
a distant colony to administer, they were not a little perplexed as to how to manage it. And the problem was
further complicated by the death of James and the acces-
sion of Charles in 1625. The king could do what he liked
with his own, as there was neither law nor precedent determining the treatment of a colony, but the fact that the
company in London had authorized the granting of a
popular assembly to its plantation was no sufficient reason
why the king should do the same. The matter was debated
at some length, but the course of events that followed is
far from clear. Either from apathy, indecision, or deliberate purpose, or perhaps with the intention of meeting the
strongly expressed wishes of the colony—for it is well
known that the government of Charles I was favorably
disposed toward the king's dominion of Virginia—the
system of popular representation was allowed to continue,
and the principle was firmly established—a principle of
far-reaching importance in British colonization—that a

royal colony should be self-governing, and should have a governor and council appointed in England and a popular assembly chosen by the electors—freemen or freeholders—in America. Though self-government was in no sense democratic government, and though popular interest in lawmaking was never very keen during colonial times, nevertheless the very presence of a popular assembly in a royal British colony in America was a factor of tremendous consequence in the development of American political ideas.

That which happened in Virginia happened elsewhere also, but under other conditions. In the charter of each proprietary colony—in the same instrument which erected the territory into a seignory and placed at its head "a true and absolute lord"—was introduced the provision, seemingly of small moment at the time, that the proprietor should have the power to make laws with the advice and assent of the "freeholders," "freemen," or "free inhabitants," as the phrases go. Out of the meeting thus gathered, under the stimulus of Virginia's example, and in response to the new ideas about government that were beginning to find voice in England during the period of Puritan revolution and rule, there arose the popular assemblies of Maryland, the Jerseys, the Carolinas, and Pennsylvania. In New England, where the Plymouth colony began as a self-governing civil and religious community and where Massachusetts and Connecticut started as religious Puritan commonwealths—self-governing, separatistic, and exclusive—we have to reckon with the church organization and political ideas of the Puritans, ideas already germinating in England but given freer opportunity of growth in the virgin land of America. The fact that Massachusetts was a local governing corporation on American soil, though its franchise was a mockery from a modern point of view, gave assurance of the eventual development of a self-governing system there on a more liberal representative basis. Connecticut, the most isolated of all the colonies from the world outside, and, with the exception of Rhode Island, the only completely self-governed colony in America during the colonial period, began as a political and religious Utopia, based on Hooker's dictum that the foundation of authority should lie in the free consent of the people. While it proved impossible to apply in practice a principle so far ahead of its time, nevertheless the presence among the colonies of one of their number governing itself in all parts of its organization, without serious interference from England, was a factor of importance to which considerable weight must be given. In 1691, when New York obtained the right to call a popular assembly, the last of the colonies which had been settled in the seventeenth century secured a government based on the Virginia model. Thus, by the beginning of the eighteenth century, every British colony in America had a representative assembly elected under a limited popular suffrage. As may be seen by studying the legislative history of Nova Scotia and the Floridas in the later period, the fact was accepted in England that a British colony, if it were to attract settlers and to attain the objects sought for in its promotion, had to be granted a certain measure of self-government. There was nothing either philanthropic or specially broad-minded in the granting of self-government to a royal colony, for the principle underlying it partook of the nature of a business proposition.

Background of the Revolution

In time, these representative assemblies increased the number and scope of their powers, and in the West Indies as well as on the American continent they opposed the feudal and royal powers wielded by the executive part of the government, and began to claim for themselves all the privileges and functions of the House of Commons in England. In Maryland, from 1660 to 1689, the struggle lay between the proprietor and the popular element. The former was attempting to run the government as a good deal of a family affair and was invoking a divine right of proprietors, which in some ways was even worse than a divine right of kings; whereas the latter was mutinous and given to faction and objected to those in office, on the ground that they were "proud and malicious" and sought "the utter ruin of the poor man." In the Carolinas, whose proprietors lived in England and in later years showed themselves incompetent and helpless, the struggle focused upon the famous Fundamental Constitutions of Locke, which at four several times were sent to South Carolina, and which, though accepted by individuals for the sake of their land titles, were rejected four times by the assembly there. In Pennsylvania trouble began soon after the English revolution of 1689 and was largely due to Penn's really extraordinary attempt to set up a liberal, Sydney-esque form of government under a charter that was mediæval in character. Penn met his match in David Lloyd, the champion of the assembly against the proprietary prerogatives, and lost the battle in 1701, when he was compelled to grant a "Charter of Privileges" that established the supremacy of a representative assembly in Pennsylvania.

With the close of this struggle—one of the most interesting in the constitutional history of the colonial period—feudal privilege, as a feature of government, may be said to have passed away in America; and thereafter the issue, both in the proprietary and in the royal colonies, took on the more modern form of executive authority versus popular control. Under this guise the outcome was far less certain, for the royal prerogative was an integral part of the British constitution and not an anachronism, as were the mediæval proprietary privileges. Though the assemblies did not deny the legality of the prerogative, as exercised in America through royal and proprietary appointees, yet they encroached upon it constantly in matters concerning their own organization, numbers, membership, duration of sitting, the appointment of judges, and, most important of all, the control of the finances, which, without a budget system of any kind, they managed as a rule very badly.

Even as early as 1705, Attorney-General Northey of England, in an unguarded moment, expressed the opinion that a colonial assembly partook of the nature of an English parliament; and in 1722 the elder Dulany, Lord Baltimore's attorney-general, in a letter to the governor, took it as a matter of course that the rules governing the summons of parliament at home applied equally well to the provincial assemblies in America. The assemblies themselves had already demonstrated the truth of both of these statements. In 1697 the Maryland lower house had declared in formal utterance that "this general assembly was in like nature of the parliament of England as to this province"; and in both the West Indies and on the American continent the legislative bodies gradually took on parliamentary form and reproduced in all essential details the procedure and privileges of the House of Commons. Though differing in many particulars among themselves, they tended toward uniformity of practice, especially in the proprietary and royal provinces, and we find the speaker with his mace and gown, the sergeant-at-arms with his staff, and the chaplain, the clerk, and the doorkeeper. In Maryland and Virginia, at least, we see the speaker "disabling" himself in true English fashion on presentation to the governor—a practice John Randolph refused to follow at a later time in Virginia; and we meet with the usual course pursued in the reading of bills, and, as far as conditions allowed, in the rules of etiquette employed in addressing the house. Proceedings were secret, and not until after the middle of the century were strangers admitted to hear debates. Only in the payment of members (except in South Carolina, Georgia, and Barbadoes, where the members were not paid) did the assemblies of the royal colonies depart from English practice, to which, in all other respects, a majority of them conformed as closely as they could. They claimed through the speaker the usual privileges of a parliamentary body, as "essentially necessary to the constitution of a free assembly" (for so the speaker phrased it in Barbadoes); and they protested and punished, whenever these privileges were violated, with an insistence and a dignity not surpassed by the House of Commons at home. They demanded and exercised, generally with royal approval, full control over their own members, in matters of admission, qualifications, and expulsion; the swearing-in of members; the punishment of absent members; and other powers that were necessary for the orderly conduct of legislative business. Only in regard to an increase of members did the king insist on his prerogative rights, and no colony was expected to add to the numbers of its assembly without the king's consent.

In Pennsylvania the assembly seems to have transgressed in these respects at the outset and to have been encouraged in so doing by Penn in his evident desire to model his government after that of king, lords, and commons. The name "House of Commons" appears in the records of Virginia as early as 1645 and in those of Maryland in 1649. In the Carolinas and the Bahamas, the proprietors themselves, in their instructions to their governors, called the assemblies "parliaments"; and in South Carolina the term "Commons House" or "Commons House of Assembly" early came into use. In 1659 and 1660 the assemblies of Virginia and Maryland, following English Puritan precedent, assumed essentially the position of a supreme legislative body; but in 1666, when the Maryland assembly seemed inclined to make a similar claim, the proprietary council countered by asserting that its powers ran no higher than those of the "common council of the City of London." In the royal colonies, the representatives of the crown, though sometimes conceding the privilege as a right, evidently in the hope of avoiding a quarrel, at other times adhered with the utmost strictness to the letter of their instructions and refused to recognize the assemblies' pretensions. In writing to the assembly of Nevis, the governor of the Leeward Islands said, "I cannot notice any comparison between you and the House of Commons"; and Hunter of New York in 1711 assumed the rôle of a prophet, when he warned the secretary of state that the assembly of that province was stretching its claims "even beyond what they were imagined to be in England"; and should the council, "by the same rule, lay claim to the rights and privileges of a House of Peers," then a body politic would exist in America "coördinate with and consequently independent of the Great Council of the Realm."

As time went on, the assemblies came to look on these rights and privileges as a part of their historical heritage, inherent in themselves as representative bodies of people; and they asserted, to quote from a Jamaican protest, that under the common law "no instruction from king or minister could abridge or annihilate their right to them." That these assemblies were going far beyond their functions as provincial councils appears not only in their claims of privilege and encroachments upon the powers of the governors, but also in their passing, as in the case of Maryland, an act of attainder—an exercise of legislative and judicial authority that belonged only to the highest court of the realm, the High Court of Parliament; or, as in the case of Massachusetts, an act of amnesty, which was something the House of Commons would not have presumed to do in the face of the king's control of the pardoning power.

One may not wonder, under the circumstances, that the Board of Trade, the Privy Council, British ministers, and legal advisers, refused to recognize the claims of the colonial assemblies to powers coequal with those of parliament or should have persisted in their refusal to do so down to the very eve of the Revolution. In 1772 the attorney-general of England, in a report which was approved by the Privy Council and its committee, having first declared that the assembly of St. Christopher had "corrupted its own constitution by affecting a power which they had not, analogous and coequal to that of the House of Commons in Great Britain," advised the king to instruct his governor "to keep his assembly within the legal bounds of a provincial council and to hinder them from usurping authorities inconsistent with the peace and good government of the island." That which was true of the West Indies was true of the continental colonies also. There could be no compromise between the view of the highest executive and legal authorities in England, on one hand, that the colonial assemblies, after one hundred and fifty years of growth and experience, were still merely provincial councils, possessed of limited and inferior powers, and the view of the colonists, on the other hand, that their assemblies had all the privileges of the House of Commons and, with some limitations, all the powers exercised by the parliament in Great Britain. These differences were irreconcilable, and the significance lies not in the fact of the conflict between the executive and legislative branches of the government —that is as old as assemblies themselves and is always with us—nor in the fact that a monarchical form of government was arrayed against one that was popular in character, though this was one of the fundamental points at issue; but in the existence in every colony of a miniature house of commons which was exercising full powers over legislation, membership, and finance, and claiming legislative equality with the highest legislative body of the realm. Such a claim affected the very constitution of the British empire itself, for it asserted that the empire was not a single state made up of a mother country and her dependencies, but rather a group of states equal in status, with coördinate legislatures and a common king.

Background of the Revolution

This view of the constitution, based on actual conditions, was common enough in the colonies before the Revolution, and was apparently in the minds of those who were responsible for the form in which the Declaration of Independence was cast. Franklin and Samuel Adams held it. The people of Windham (Connecticut) believed in it, when they declared in town meeting "that neither the Parliament of Britain, nor the Parliament of France, nor any other Parliament but that which sits supreme in our own Province has a right to lay taxes on us for the purpose of raising a revenue." Madison voiced it as a widespread conviction, when he wrote in 1800 that "the fundamental principle of the Revolution was that the colonies were coördinate members with each other and Great Britain of an empire united by a common executive sovereign, and that the legislative power was maintained to be as complete in each American parliament as in the British parliament." But no British lawyer or member of the governing class in Great Britain could have considered such a doctrine as anything but a complete subversion of all existing constitutional ideas and a menace to the organization of the British empire. Yet it represented the facts in the case more truly than did the British official opinion. Unfortunately, it was the British official and lawyer and not the colonial statesman who determined the attitude of the crown and its advisers during that critical period of controversy which led up to the events of 1776.

British statesmen and members of parliament did not understand the situation in America, because they knew too little about colonial affairs and were blind to the significance of that which came to their attention. Seemingly they were unable to sound the depths or take the measure of what was happening in their own colonies. An English correspondent in 1776 wrote of the members of parliament, "it is surprising how ignorant some of them are of trade and America." The secretary of state, who should have found time for a careful and intelligent consideration of colonial questions, was occupied with problems of war and diplomacy, and immersed in matters of politics and patronage; and though he tried by means of letters and "answers to queries," notably in 1766, 1767, and 1773, to obtain information, he never was a true colonial secretary, even after 1768 when a third member of the secretariat was appointed for colonial business. Had Halifax been made secretary of state for the colonies, as was very nearly done in 1757, more than ten years before Hillsborough was appointed to that office—a much inferior man at a much more difficult time—affairs might have turned out differently. Halifax had some knowledge of the colonies and was in sympathy with them; Hillsborough had little knowledge and was narrow-minded and obstinate.

The Board of Trade, much better informed about the colonies than either the secretary of state or the Privy Council, exercised very little direct influence, because it had no power to act on its own initiative and was frequently interfered with by the higher executive authorities or by parliament. It was a thoroughly mercantilist body, which insisted on the most rigid enforcement of the navigation acts; deemed "nothing so essentially necessary to the preservation of His Majtys Governt in the American provinces, as the careful and strikt maintenance of the just prerogative"; and declared wholly improper the passing of laws in the colonies for encouraging manufactures. It maintained that such manufactures interfered with those of Great Britain; and that "the great expense which this country has been and is still at for the defence and protection of the colonies, while they on the other hand contribute little or nothing to the taxes with which it is burthen'd, gives it a just claim to restrain them in such attempts." Such recommendations of policy as the board made were based on the habits and traditions of its own office, and were generally limited either to minor questions or to matters of detail; those concerned with larger issues show as little vision as do the recommendations of the executive officials themselves. Its members failed utterly to grasp the fact that the colonies were no longer plantations to be exploited for commercial profit, or inferior political entities limited in their functions to the making of by-laws and the issuing of ordinances. They failed to realize that these old-time plantations in America were no longer corporations but had grown up and become states in the making—self-conscious and self-reliant political communities. It would seem as if some inkling of the real situation might have penetrated the official British mind, but ignorance, stubbornness, and lack of imagination combined to prevent the men in office from understanding and interpreting the events that were taking place year by year under their own observation. They viewed the colonial world not as something to be approached and judged for its own sake, but rather as something subordinate and supplemental, to be dealt with only from the standpoint of Great Britain's own needs and her relations with the European Continent.

British Colonies in America

At the same time it must be said that the colonists were equally ignorant of much that was going on in the larger world of European rivalry or were unable to comprehend the significance of events that were passing before their own eyes. They ignored the important issues that Great Britain had at stake. Even if they comprehended them—and some did—they were impatient of consequences, fearing lest British success would mean greater limitation of their own opportunities than before. But like mother, like daughter. In concentrating all their efforts on the one great task of preserving and extending the advantages they had won, the colonists responded instinctively to the separatist motives within them, and in so doing laid the foundations of a new republic, a great self-governing state, destined in time to become one of the leading powers of the earth. At the same time Great Britain responded to the ideals and tendencies that were to make her a great "Commonwealth of Nations," and in principle, at least, was as much justified in acting according to her needs and impulses as were the colonists in following theirs. Justice can be done her only when we accept the fact that her policy was founded, not on hostility to the colonies,—an attitude that would have been suicidal and destructive of her own best interests, as she saw them,—but on what seemed to her the absolute necessity of adapting colonial resources—which after all were her own resources—to her own imperative needs and advantages.

Turning now to that part of our subject which constitutes the third most important aspect of the colonial relationship with the mother country, namely, the attitude of the colonies toward crown and parliament, we approach a difficult topic heretofore inadequately studied and but im-

Background of the Revolution

perfectly understood. The evidence at our disposal for the study of sentiment and opinion in the colonies is very limited in character—its sources being largely official documents, newspapers, pamphlets, and a small body of scattered material of a purely private nature—yet what we have enables us to reach certain conclusions that are approximately correct. Colonial subordination to the authority of the mother country was no legal fiction, for the vast majority of the colonists accepted it as the normal condition of their lives. This was notably true after 1713, when colonial habits of business and opportunities for profit had become more settled, and people had adapted themselves to the requirements and advantages of the British system. Rigid though this system seemed to be in law, it was, in practice, flexible and sufficiently adjustable to the needs of the colonists to enable them to move easily and freely within its boundaries and, in the main, to prosper under the conditions it imposed. Complaints there were, as always there must be under any system of regulation and control; but these complaints have more to do with the way in which the system worked than with the principle of subordination which it involved. That constantly a half-conscious effort was being made by the colonists to loosen the bonds of dependence admits of no doubt, for independence, in many directions other than political, was achieved long before actual revolt began. But during the years before 1763 the colonists thought of themselves and called themselves the "fellow subjects" of the king's subjects at home, and, as a rule, were too much occupied in making a living to question the advantages of the British connection, or to doubt the legality of a system that offered so many opportunities for evasion. If we argue forward from the restlessness of the seventeenth century or backward from the discontent of the years after 1763, we can easily make ourselves believe that the colonists were in a chronic state of dissatisfaction with the restrictions imposed upon them by the British crown and parliament; but, in reality, in proportion to the total population, there were fewer among them who deliberately broke the laws that England enacted than there are among the citizens of the United States to-day who are deliberately breaking the Volstead Act; and fewer still openly raised their voices against England's interference in their affairs than opposed the adoption of the Federal Constitution in 1787 and 1788, or are to-day expressing their fears of a centralized Federal government. Those most affected by the navigation acts and other constraining measures were the merchants and men of business, and not the agricultural population; yet it was the "embattled farmer," and not the "embattled merchant," whose shot was heard round the world. Other causes, therefore, than the navigation acts and restrictive measures must be found for our Revolution.

He would be a poor historian indeed who believed that the colonists thought of themselves as living in independent communities, awaiting the time when as ripened fruit they should separate from the parent stem. In view of the facts which are easily accessible, it is difficult to understand how supporters have been found for the theory that the executive power in England, "the king's headship of the empire," was merely "an ornamental constitutional feature." Without exception, the officials in the royal colonies—which eventually made up five-sixths of the whole

group—received their appointments and instructions from
the crown, either directly from the king or one of the
executive departments in England, or, indirectly, from the
king's governor in the colonies under the provincial seal.
They looked to England for their authority, and, according to the current view of office-holding in the eighteenth
century, they considered themselves responsible only to
God and the king. All commissions, instructions, warrants,
mandamuses, and the like came either from Whitehall
or from Doctors' Commons, were drawn up there by the
proper authorities, and were issued in precisely the same
way as similar documents were issued to officials at home.
The vice-admiralty courts in the colonies were presided
over by judges commissioned by the High Court of Admiralty under warrant from the crown and exercised a
jurisdiction considerably wider than that of the same
courts in England. The customs officials were appointed
for some forty-nine different ports and rivers by the
Treasury and the Commissioners of Customs. As the British organization in America widened and became better
systematized many other functionaries,—surveyors, general agents, and superintendents,—whose business it was to
watch over large sections of territory, in the interest of defense, navigation, woods, and Indian affairs, or to keep an
eye on the rights of the crown and parliament, were created
from time to time by the home government. In the eighteenth century there were always some British troops in
colonial barracks, and a few British frigates in American
waters to guard the coast and prevent illegal trading. Captains looked to the Admiralty for their convoys and Mediterranean passes, and governors and assemblies applied to

the Board of Ordnance for the guns and ammunition needed for their harbor forts. Colonial officials—civil, military, and naval—corresponded with the Secretary of State and the Board of Trade, with the Admiralty, Treasury, and Commissioners of Customs. They also sent over statistics, copies of laws, and information about colonial affairs, and made it possible for the various British authorities to inform themselves, if they wished to do so, regarding events and conditions in the different parts of the colonial world.

In their turn, the executive authorities in England frequently stretched a restraining hand over the colonies, restricting their freedom of action, whenever they seemed to be trespassing on the higher rights of crown and mother country. That the colonies objected in practice to the exercise of some parts of the royal prerogative—particularly in matters of legislation and legislative procedure— is true; but it is important to note that none of them ever denied its legality. The Privy Council, acting on the recommendations of the Board of Trade and its legal advisers, disallowed all colonial laws which encroached on the king's powers, affected the allegiance of any of the king's subjects, contravened an act of parliament or a convention of the common law, or seemed to impair, in any way, the interests of British merchants and British trade in America. The king's "royal will and pleasure," vague though it sometimes was and always undefined, existed as an integral part of the British constitution and could not legally be infringed. In British eyes, the statute and common law of England represented the highest attainment of human wisdom and experience, and could be departed from only in domestic concerns and then but rarely; and the interests of colonial trade, in the face of the rivalry with France and other nations, were paramount over all other considerations. Colonial laws offending in any of these particulars were disallowed very often by the Privy Council in all the colonies, except Connecticut and Rhode Island, and even there in three instances. Such disallowance, and the delays attending its exercise, occasionally caused hardship and confusion and offended colonial susceptibilities; but disallowance itself was a perfectly legal act of royal regulation and found its justification, not only in the king's constitutional rights under the common law but even more in the proneness of colonial assemblies to pass laws, either bad in themselves or inimical to the welfare of British merchants trading with America. In fact, the colonists themselves sometimes appealed to the king to disallow what they believed were injurious acts passed by their neighbors, and however much those of a particular colony may have disliked the disallowance when applied to their own assembly, they did not object to having the process applied to the assemblies of other colonists that happened to be rivals in some given field.

But whereas the relations with the king were thus carefully defined and clearly understood by the colonists, those with parliament were very unsettled. The reason for this is clear, because parliament itself was growing and changing and demanding more and more power. Everyone agreed that the colonies were the king's, but the notion that parliament could legislate for all the king's dominions had hardly become, at the time of the settlement, a maxim of the English lawyer. The Commonwealth act of 1649,

which asserted the supreme authority of parliament over
the dominions beyond the seas, had no validity after the
restoration of Charles II in 1660, and thus in no way influenced the policy of its successors; so perhaps the earliest
enunciation of the principle is to be found in Penn's charter, which contains the implication that parliament might
tax the colony should it wish to do so. But by 1765 Penn-
sylvanians were able to explain away that clause of the
charter to their own satisfaction. "I cannot think," wrote
William Allen to Thomas Penn in that year, "that when
it is said in the royal charter that no taxes are to be laid
on us but by act of parliament gives any right to tax us
except there was a right lodged in the parliament before
that charter; for if the king's declaration could deprive us
of what we conceive to be our right, viz., being taxed by
our own representatives, we never had the right of freemen. In case parliament had not that right prior to the
royal charter no declaration of the crown could empower
them to lay taxes on us." In matters of special pleading,
few could surpass the men of Pennsylvania and Connecticut, when they were defending the interests of their respective colonies. That a right to tax the colonies had been
lodged in parliament before 1681 would be exceedingly
difficult to prove, and unless it were proved Pennsylvania
could present a very strong case. But the question was not
raised at all until 1765 and there is nothing to show that
earlier writers thought it serious enough to call for comment, because, as is stated in the preface to Governor Bernard's *Letters on the Trade and Government of America*,
published in 1774, parliament up to that time "was scarce
allowed to have anything to do with [the colonies] and

interfered very little with their government." Governor Evans, in his controversy with the Pennsylvania assembly in 1707, declared that "the English parliament [had] all original power, while the province had only specified granted powers and nothing [could] be done beyond them." To which opinion the assembly replied that although all original power lay in parliament, even specified granted powers had "necessary incidentals to this action, in the form of implied additional powers." Thus early was the doctrine of implied powers introduced into our constitutional history. Even as late as 1764, Governor Fitch of Connecticut could write to Richard Jackson, "For these reasons we have avoided all pretence of objection against the authority or power of the parliament as the supreme legislature of all the king's dominions, and have therefore endeavored only to show that the exercise of such power in that particular instance or in like cases will take away part of our antient privileges." Evidently Governor Fitch was not familiar with that doctrine of coördinate legislatures and a common king which got so well rooted in the next decade. It would be interesting to know how early that doctrine began to take shape in colonial minds.

The colonists of the eighteenth century were not ignorant of the changes that had come upon the British constitution as a result of the Puritan Revolution and the Revolution of 1689. Thousands of Englishmen settled in America after these events, and hundreds of the colonists visited England in the eighteenth century and watched the course of English constitutional history. Some of them studied at the Inns of Court; more of them heard the debates in the House of Commons and the House of Lords, and, by following the current political gossip of the day, acquired a knowledge of prevailing political opinions regarding parliament's competency to legislate for the colonies. No one can say that the constitutional ideas which the first settlers brought with them were handed on as an unchanging inheritance to the later generations, or that colonial leaders knew no version of the English constitution save that which prevailed in the days of the Stuarts. Well informed colonists were quite aware that during the eighteenth century parliament had risen to a position of influence superior to that of king and council and that after 1740 the House of Commons had become the most powerful and assertive member of the legislative group in England.

Likewise, the colonists had been familiar for a long while with acts of parliament concerning themselves, not only with those that regulated their trade and commerce, but with the very few others that affected their domestic activities. They early evolved the idea that such legislation, to be binding, should be accompanied by representation on their own part in the English parliament. It is to be noted that in the years before 1684, Massachusetts taxed the non-freemen of the colony without giving them representation in the assembly that taxed them; that Virginia and Maryland taxed the Quakers; and that the English inhabitants of St. Christopher taxed the French in the island without giving them the right to vote. Yet Massachusetts denied as early as 1673, that parliament had the right to extend the navigation acts to New England, because the colonies there had not been represented in the parliament that passed them. Very rarely was Massachusetts, as a Puritan commonwealth, willing to adopt the elementary principle of commutative justice in her relations with others. Apparently she had forgotten that her own Winthrop once acknowledged that the colony was "virtually" represented in parliament, by means of the burgesses or knights of the shire in which the royal manor of East Greenwich was situated, of which manor, constructively at least, the lands of the Massachusetts Bay Company were a part. Before the end of the seventeenth century there were others, too, who thought that "no law of England ought to be in force and binding to them without their own consent," and "foolishly" said, to quote Governor Nicholson, that "they have no representative sent from themselves to the parliament of England" and look upon "all laws made in England that put any restraint upon them to be a great hardship." Opinions of this sort were more common during the years from 1689 to 1713 than they were in the fifty years that followed. In 1708 Robert Quary reported that the assemblies of Pennsylvania, New Jersey, and New York would not "allow of" the laws of England, unless the queen would permit them "to send their representatives to sett in the parliament of Great Britain." Again in 1707 and 1710 there were those in New Jersey and Virginia who protested against the imposition by parliament of a letter postage—which they construed as a form of taxation—on the same ground of not being represented in parliament. But others of the colonists, then and afterwards, denied that postage was a tax, asserting that it was a form of payment for a service rendered, and that no one was obliged to pay it unless he wished. The question of representation does not appear to

have been raised again until after 1763, and the objections
to a letter postage were dropped altogether, except by a
few supersensitive souls here and there at the time of the
Stamp Act.

There was always a certain amount of inconsistency in
colonial points of view, and one must not look upon individual expressions of opinion as binding upon a whole
people; but, generally speaking, it is safe to say that in
the eighteenth century before 1763 the colonists did not
seriously oppose the extension of English law to the colonies and made no denial of parliament's right to legislate
for them. In the royal colonies the rule prevailed that
"where the law of the colony was silent, that of England
was to be pursued"; or, as North Carolina phrased it in
1711, "the laws of England are the laws of this government, so far as they are compatible with our ways of living
and trade." Maryland went so far as to assert that no custom of the country was to stand that was contrary to the
laws of England; and in 1704, when her assembly said—
as if it were a commonly accepted fact needing no demon-
stration—that "the laws of England supercede all our
laws," no one made reply to the contrary. In 1728 the
elder Dulany argued at length and in print to prove the
"right of the people of Maryland to the benefit of all
the English laws, of every kind, that have been instituted
for the preservation and security of the subject's liberty."
Even in Rhode Island, as Governor Cranston stated in
1709, the laws of England were "approved of and pleaded, to all intents and purposes, without it be some perticular
acts for the prudential affairs of the colony and not repugnant to the laws of England." Only in the religious Puri-

Background of the Revolution

tan commonwealths of Massachusetts and Connecticut, where the desire to maintain their religious and political independence overruled all other considerations, was the parliamentary statute largely ignored and the assertion made that "they were not bound in conscience" to obey the laws of England. Yet even the law of these colonies was based on the English common law and had been from the beginning. Connecticut in the eighteenth century added some parts of the statute law of England to her own "law of God and the rule of righteousness"; and Massachusetts, when it suited her convenience, as during the administration of Andros, laid claim to the very laws of England which formerly she had repudiated. Indeed, at that time her leaders made such a vigorous demand for all the benefits of Magna Carta and other "documents of English liberty" that Dudley had to remind them, in accordance with their own earlier opinions on the subject, that "they must not think that the laws of England followed them to the ends of the earth."

Although the colonies, through their agents or others, frequently petitioned against the passage by parliament of bills that applied directly to them or mentioned them as subject to the provisions laid down, they raised no protest against such bills on the ground of illegality. They never objected, as far as I know, to the remarkable assertion in the navigation act of 1696 that any laws, by-laws, usages, or customs in the colonies contrary to the act "or to any other law hereafter to be made in this kingdom, so far as such law shall relate to or mention the plantations," should be illegal, null, and void. Had the colonists really been opposed to parliamentary interference at that time, this very sweeping provision might easily have aroused resentment. Except for reasons of equity and justice, no remonstrance appears to have been made to the very serious bills of 1701 and 1706 which were designed to bring the proprietary and corporate colonies under the control of the crown; or to a later threat of the Board of Trade in 1721 to call parliament to its aid if the assemblies of these same private colonies did not cease their efforts to encroach upon the prerogative of the crown in America. The colonists in general accepted as a matter of course the woolen act of 1699; the coinage act of 1708; the post-office act of 1710; the six-penny duty act of 1729; the debt act and hat act of 1732; the calendar, iron, and paper money acts of 1751; and all measures that touched woods and naval stores and encouraged the raising of raw materials in New England. In fact, during these earlier years they were less concerned with the question of constitutional legality than with the problem how to evade or ward off, without danger to themselves, the royal order or the parliamentary statute. They never denied the right of parliament to assume by statute the functions of the Privy Council, even when that statute applied to the king's dominions beyond the seas.

Quite the contrary. There were colonies that were ready and even eager to invoke the aid of parliament when it was worth their while to do so. For instance, Increase Mather was willing that the charter of the Puritan commonwealth of Massachusetts should be restored in 1689 by means of a rider attached to an act of parliament; and when that body dissolved without action he was discouraged because "a whole year's Sisyphean labor" had gone for nothing. Another example is the case of Leisler and Milborn in

New York, who under an act of Henry VIII (25 Henry VIII, c. 8, §2) had been condemned and executed for refusing to plead. In 1695 the adherents of Leisler obtained by act of parliament a reversal of his attainder. In 1697 the agents of New York, in a petition to the Board of Trade, urged the appointment by act of parliament of "a prudent and experienced general over all the military forces of the continent," without which, they said, "obedience cannot rationally be expected." Both Connecticut and Barbadoes, one in 1728 and the other in 1731, preferred an act of parliament to an order in council as more likely to accomplish to the advantage of the colony a particular object desired. Many a colonial statute was modeled directly and intentionally after some one or other of the acts of parliament, though generally it was not considered necessary to insert a reference to that fact in the wording of the act itself. Colonial lawyers in their briefs and colonial judges in their decisions from the bench constantly cited acts of parliament, from Magna Carta down to the statutes of their own day, to support their arguments and findings; and it is at least significant that the colonists claimed all the benefits of the Habeas Corpus Act of 1679, even though English lawyers denied their right to the particular privileges of the act because the colonies were not specifically mentioned in it. The benefits of *habeas corpus* under the common law had always been enjoyed in America.

It was a current legal opinion in the eighteenth century, formally approved by the attorney general of England in 1729, that acts passed after settlement began in which the colonists were not named, could not be enforced in the colonies, unless adopted by the local assemblies as their law. But this procedure was not consistently followed, for as a writer said in 1726, "Judges who by their education are but indifferently qualified for that service sometimes allow the force of particular statutes and at other times reject the whole, especially if the Bench is inclinable to be partial, which too frequently happens in those new and unsettled countries." That colonial officials and lawyers were often puzzled by these legal aphorisms appears from their remarks. Said Governor Codrington of the Leeward Islands in 1701: "I have seen it under my Lord Chief Justice Pemberton's hand that no acts of parliament are of force here in which the plantations are not nam'd. If it be said (as it often is) that those acts only wch. are declarative of the common law are of force here, who shall define in particular what those acts are? To give a true judgment in any difficulty of this kind wch. may arise upon trials, will require a much deeper skill in the ancient usages of the kingdom than most of our judges are at leisure to acquire. I may suppose, with all respect to them, that few of them read Bracton, Britton, or the Year Books. If acts of parliament be not of force here, but where the plantations are named, then by what authority have our judges left the measures of the common law and proceeded by acts of parliament in trials of treasons, murders, etc.? How can our judges deny benefit of clergy to one convict of murder, since criminals are ousted of the benefit by the statute law? I hope it will not be said that acts that contradict the common law are declarative of the common law." John Randolph, attorney general of Virginia, seemed equally perplexed, when he wrote in 1735: "I can't help observing a mighty weakness of the lawyers of New York in blindly following a common error in relation to the statutes of England being in force there. The common law must be the only rule, and if we wade into the statutes, no man can tell what the law is. It is certain that all of them can't bind and to know which do was always above my capacity."

Thus it is evident that during the colonial period, no one knew certainly what was law and what was not in the colonies. Some took the ground that the law of England was in force, and when that could not be applied, then the laws of the colonies were to be obeyed. Others believed that the colonial laws had precedence, and that those of England were operative only when colonial law was wanting. Still others contended for a judicious combination of the two, but even they were at variance as to the character of the ingredients. Some admitted only such statutes as were passed in England before the first settlement; others approved of all later statutes in which the colonies were named; while a few argued in favor of any statute that was capable of application because of similarity of conditions. Unanimity was never reached on any of these points. Colonial opinion ranged from denial by the governors of Connecticut that English statute law had any validity unless formally adopted by the colony itself, to the contention of Dulany that all English law, common and statute, had place in America. The situation was further complicated by the necessity of discriminating between a royal instruction, an order in council, and a parliamentary statute. British officials in the colonies insisted that a governor's instruction was mandatory, while members of the colonial assemblies took the ground that it was recommendatory only, except in its application to the governor himself; but they generally agreed that an order in council and an act of parliament directly referring to the colonies were obligatory. Many a lively dispute arose in the efforts which were made to decide these questions.

The one thing to be kept in mind is that the right of parliament to legislate for the colonies was not expressly denied by the colonists themselves before 1765; for although they often succeeded in thwarting the royal will and evading the acts of parliament, they accepted their colonial status up to that time with a reasonable measure of equanimity and content, neither denying their dependence on the crown nor refusing to acknowledge the right of parliament to enact measures that were designed to bind them in matters of purely domestic concern. Nor did they raise the issue of parliamentary sovereignty until the events of the pre-Revolutionary period made it necessary for them to discover a constitutional argument that would serve as a pretext for revolt. John Adams's assertion, made in 1775, that the authority of parliament was never admitted as of right in the internal affairs of the colonies is, like other of Adams's statements, not in accord with the facts of the case. Over against it may be set the remark of Thomas Pownall, a former governor of Massachusetts and one of the fairest of the British critics, who had every reason to know the situation in America. He declared in 1764 that the claim of freedom from the authority of parliament was of very recent growth. "I do not believe," he wrote, "that there ever was an instance when the principle of the supreme legislature's power to raise monies by taxes throughout the realm of Great Britain was ever called in question, either in the assemblies or in the courts of the colonies; nor did I ever hear of any book, treatise, or even news-paper essay that ever until this moment even moved it as a question of right. However general this claim of exemption from being taxed by act of parliament may have become of late; however suddenly this wild plant forced by an artificial fire may have sprung up and spread itself, it is neither the natural produce nor growth of America. The colonists in their sober senses know too well the necessary powers of government; they have too well considered the relation which they as colonists bear to the realm of Great Britain; their true and real liberties and charter rights are dearer to them than that they should hazard them by grasping after shadows and phantoms."

As a basis for generalizations regarding the colonies as a whole, too much dependence has hitherto been placed upon the early attitude of Massachusetts and Connecticut toward English statute law. There is no doubt that before 1765 many of the colonists in general, particularly those of a legal turn of mind, felt uncertain and perplexed as to the status and weight of parliamentary law in America, but they never deliberately denied its authority as they sometimes denied the mandatory character of the king's instructions. In fact, before 1763 the king's prerogative, because it was exercised more frequently through the commissions and instructions to the royal governors and stood as a persistent obstacle in the path leading to a popular control of local affairs, was disliked much more than was the statute of parliament. Such opposition as existed to an act of parliament came, as a rule, from those who were concerned for its effect upon their personal and class interests and found in its provisions some menace, as they thought, to their own well being. Even the vigorous protests of the New England merchants against the Sugar Act of 1764 do not contain a single word that can be construed as a denial of the legality of the act itself. They declared it to be "highly injurious and detrimental to all his Majesty's North American colonies in general" and to their own colony in particular, but not once did they say that parliament had no legal right to pass such a measure. Only after several acts had been passed, of a nature, as they saw it, prejudicial to the welfare of the colonists, did the idea of constitutional illegality enter the minds of the colonists and control their utterances and actions. After 1765, in increasing numbers, they began to deny the power of parliament, just as they were beginning to take stronger ground against the authority of the royal prerogative; but in both instances they were defying a constitution to which previously they had considered themselves bound to conform.

The American intellectuals may have been legally right, as Professor McIlwain contends, in thus denying the validity of a parliamentary statute to bind the colonies, but the fact remains that they did not find it out until the question of taxation was reached and the menace of parliamentary aggression had begun to warn them of dangers to come. The "rightness" or "wrongness" of the matter, though of great significance in the history of opinion touching the organization of the British empire, has but an academic interest in its relation to the progress of our revolution. The colonists would have gone ahead with their revolt, regardless of the conclusions of the intellectuals, for the impulses behind that movement did not originate in the question of parliamentary right. John Adams was an admirable logician, but, as Professor McIlwain also says, "logic is not all of life." The spirit of revolt was abroad in the land before October 14, 1774, when was adopted the fourth article of the "Declaration" of the first Continental Congress that predicated "a free and exclusive power of legislation in their several provincial legislatures . . . in all cases of taxation and internal polity." This article may have served to convince the lukewarm of the justness of their position, and to stiffen the determination of others who had already become convinced of the necessity —unavoidable as they believed it to be—of severing their connection with a government which persisted in adhering to an outworn doctrine of colonial dependency and of winning for themselves a position of political independence in harmony with their spiritual aspirations and the conditions of their social and economic life. Thomas Paine's *Common Sense* is a masterpiece of pure emotionalism, but this treatise had more influence in focusing the spirit of revolt than the writings of all the intellectuals taken together. No assertion of "right," however convincingly argued, that might have been made in America at this time, could have altered, in any particular, the belief of the majority of the members of parliament or of Englishmen generally that parliament was supreme in matters of legislation—a fact that became increasingly evident as the colonists passed from a denial of parliament's right to levy an internal tax to a denial of parliament's right to legislate for the colonies in any respect whatever. As we

shall see later, parliament's "criterion," as Professor Pol-
lard says, "was its own privilege and it had little respect
for anyone else's liberty." It would have paid no attention
to the reasoned arguments of the American writers, had
such arguments been brought before it, for it consistently
refused to consider any petitions that reflected on its constitutional powers.

Thus, in the eighteenth century, Great Britain found
herself in possession of a group of self-reliant, self-willed
colonies, composed in the main of her own flesh and blood,
and proud of the race from which they had sprung. These
colonies were advancing rapidly out of their plantation
state into that of self-governing communities, and were
growing in self-consciousness, population, and the complexity of their economic and social needs. Almost unaware
of their own strength, they accepted their position in the
British colonial world as a natural and inevitable condition
of the life in which they had been reared; and though constantly striving for a greater measure of freedom and self-
government, as they attained to larger stature, they did not
seriously contest the authority of king and parliament
before the beginning of the pre-Revolutionary era. Even
as late as December, 1765, a group of leaders, afterwards
high among those who made up the patriotic or radical
party, could say, in an endeavor to quiet rumors that were
current in England: "We find that attempts have been
made to raise a jealousy in the English nation that the
colonists were struggling for independence, than which
nothing can be more injurious. It is neither their interest,
nor have they ever shown the least disposition to be inde-

pendent of Great Britain. They have always prided themselves on being British subjects."

On the other hand, Great Britain, having acquired colonies by accident rather than intention, seemed wholly unable to prepare for their growing up by any flexible method of management and control. With characteristic opportunism, and with an eye only to the needs and obligations of the kingdom itself, her statesmen faced the problem of what to do with a colony, and how to adjust its interests to those of the mother country without higher aim than that of business profit. They began without a constructive plan of any kind; as time went on and the demands of state and nation became more insistent, they laid down certain fundamental rules, which were enforced far too often by means of temporary expedients instead of established constitutional law, properly adapted to the nature of colonial government. Finally, having elaborated a well balanced system of colonial subordination and dependence in the interest of the trade and commerce of their own kingdom, they adhered to it with a tenacity of purpose which took no account of the growth to manhood of the colonies themselves, and which eventually resulted in the American Revolution and the disruption of the British empire.

II.

The Mother Country and its Colonial Policy, 1713–1763

The Mother Country and its Colonial Policy, 1713–1763

N tracing the course of British colonial policy from 1713 to 1763, we are obliged to consider special features of the history of Great Britain and her colonies during this period of half a century. In the first place, the British colonial world was steadily growing larger and more complex. From one colony in 1607 it rose to twenty-five after 1713, and thirty-three after 1763; and as these colonies advanced rapidly in wealth and prosperity, they formed habits of self-reliance and developed methods of government that were in many ways more free, more individual, and less stereotyped than were those prevailing in the mother country at the same time. Secondly, in her foreign relations Great Britain was confronted with a constantly shifting international situation that presented new obligations and new perplexities, and demanded frequent enlargements and alterations of policy to enable her to meet, with efficiency and despatch, the various emergencies that arose. And, thirdly, the British constitution itself was undergoing far-reaching changes in form and spirit: much that was old was giving way to much that was new, old powers became vested in new hands, and authority in matters that concerned administration and control was often transient and uncertain. It is not sufficiently recognized by writers on our colonial history that during our colonial period the foreign and colonial policies of Great Britain passed through several clearly defined stages, and that her political and social order underwent a noteworthy and remarkable transformation.

The history of Europe from the sixteenth to the eighteenth centuries was strongly monarchical and national, in contrast to its imperial and unified status during the Middle Ages. The centralization prevailing under pope and emperor, never complete and rarely effective, met its doom in the rise of the maritime states of the West, among which territorial and commercial rivalry was a conspicuous factor. England's maritime rivals were first Portugal and then Spain, the former a negligible competitor, the latter the great colossus of the western world. Hostility for Spain, arising in the religious conflict of the Elizabethan era, continued down to the very eve of the Restoration, a century later. In order to loosen the hold that Spain had acquired on the West, English seamen sailed boldly into Spanish waters, capturing towns and galleons, planting settlements upon islands in the very heart of the Caribbean, and endeavoring to promote commerce in a region which Spain had claimed as peculiarly her own. Trading companies sent out ships laden with colonists and supplies, hoping thereby to obtain those tropical commodities—drugs, dyes, spices, cloths, and fruits—that the Englishmen of the day valued as scarcely inferior to gold, silver, and precious stones. In this period of western enterprise, England was not seeking empire or promoting colonies for the purpose of territorial increase. She was giving vent to the bitterness of her hatred against Spain, and at the same time was pressing for a share of those raw materials which only the warm countries of the earth could furnish abundantly, or which the cold countries could supply, but only at the cost of an unfavorable exchange either in goods or money.

Portugal as a competing rival was eliminated by means of a series of treaties with England and by the terms of the marriage settlement between Charles II and Catharine of Braganza, which reduced that country to a position of commercial vassalage. Spain finally was rendered harmless by her own administrative inefficiency, bankruptcy, and naval deterioration. But Holland, who had already crowded out Portugal from many of her points of vantage in the East and in Brazil, now entered the field, and for three-quarters of a century remained the mistress of the carrying trade in the Eastern and Western seas. Outmatched by the superior naval and mercantile skill of the Dutch people, England was compelled to adopt new strategy and to widen the scope of her naval and commercial policy. Where the Tudors, in order to avoid the decay of national shipping, had groped uncertainly toward the establishment of sea-power, the Stuarts founded and developed it and made it an aggressive instrument in British hands for the overthrow of a resourceful rival. England's organized method of extending her sea-power is seen in the famous navigation acts of 1651, 1660, 1663, and 1673, and the various regulations and appointments that accompanied and followed them, whereby her own people became the sole carriers of British commerce and appropriated and secured for England and her subjects all the emoluments arising from the trade of her own colonies. By such means she sought to wrest from the Dutch their control of sea-borne trade, and by monopolizing the colonial output she was able to add to the national stock of raw materials and to confine the importation of European goods into the colonies within routes that passed through her own ports. All the while she was striving to increase her customs receipts; to ensure the proper collection of all the royal revenues in the plantations, by extending her audit system; to augment the profits from her fisheries; and to enlarge the navy and strengthen the merchant marine, by adding to the number of seamen and multiplying the tonnage of ships. It not infrequently happened, as early as the seventeenth century, particularly in the religious Puritan commonwealths of New England, which did not want to have anything to do with the British system, that in her attempts to meet her impelling needs—as during the Andros administration—England ran athwart colonial practices and aspirations, thereby producing much friction and an enduring ill will.

After 1675, when the Dutch monopoly of the carrying trade was a thing of the past, England seemed to be advancing successfully on her way toward commercial independence and leadership. But already girding herself for the lists was a greater rival—France—who differed from England's earlier opponents in that she, as well as England, was aiming at colonial and commercial supremacy, and was dominated by an overpowering ambition to become the leading state not only in Europe but upon the ocean also. She was enlarging her territory by planting settlements for profit in the West Indies; rooting herself firmly in Canada, where the seignorial system, with its strong peasant farming stock, gave substantial body to the military régime; and finding lodgment in Louisiana and up the Mississippi to the Illinois country, which, though organ-

ized on a trading and military basis, was to no small extent
a region of villages, farmers, and wheat fields. She was
chartering trading companies for carrying on the slave
trade and the establishing of colonies; and with nervous
energy was building a merchant marine that she might be
as powerful on the sea as she had been already on the land.
She aspired to be what England was fast becoming—a
trading nation, owing its wealth, freedom, and power to
the industry of the people at home and the extensive commerce that this industry enabled it to carry on abroad. That
she might realize her desires, she was putting into operation a scheme of trade which, though more artificially
fostered, and differing in some important particulars from
that of England, was, in many of its features, identical
with that of her great antagonist. She was a rival ready to
compete with England at every point of her widening
sphere of activity and to put to the hardest test her growing powers. Thus the eighteenth century shows us two well
matched contestants, actuated by similar aims and purposes, eagerly extending their colonial area in the interest
of trade, shipping, and manufactures, and seeking the welfare, wealth, and power of their respective kingdoms.
Seemingly, in the first encounter, France more than held
her own, for in 1745 an English mercantilist pamphleteer
could say with concern that "the French commerce and
colonies, from being inferior to ours, have risen to a
dangerous superiority over us in less than half a century."

But in several fundamental respects these two antago-
nists were dissimilar. France was an absolute monarchy,
the executive powers of which were highly developed and
excessively centralized, but whose law-making functions,

Background of the Revolution

which were exercised by an estates-general, corresponding to an English parliament, remained dormant for another century. As far as its form of government was concerned, this unified French state continued unchanged during the whole of our colonial period, and because it was free from the distracting interference of a parliament or other agency limiting the prerogatives of the crown, it was admirably fitted to take prompt and efficient action in any struggle for supremacy with England. This centralized control, uniformity of plan, and unrestricted royal authority sometimes induced excessive paternalism—particularly in matters of military defense and direct supervision of the domestic concerns of her colonies—but it also made possible relief in the form of gifts, loans, land grants, and other varieties of state aid during the period of emigration and settlement, and great generosity in times of stress, when fire and hurricane destroyed houses and crops. France introduced no "enumeration" clauses into the royal arrêts and decrees which determined her commercial policy, and imposed only moderate duties on imported colonial products. The French islands of Guadeloupe, Martinique, Marie Galante, and Hispaniola were alike more fertile and less liable to exhaustion than were the British islands, and because the French African Company—unlike the Royal African Company of England—had a monopoly of the slave business, could count on a cheap and continuous supply of negro labor. Nevertheless, advantageous as the French system seemed and was, it had evil consequences, for the islands always lacked the spirit of independence and self-reliance which characterized the British islands, and never became anything more than plantation colonies growing tropical produce by means of slave labor.

On the other hand, conditions in England and her colonies were exactly the opposite of those in France. England imposed heavier restrictions upon colonial trade and levied heavier customs duties at the home ports, but she interfered rarely in the internal affairs of the colonies and concerned herself scarcely at all with matters of emigration, state aid, and maintenance. She expected the colonists to stand on their own feet and to support themselves. In 1742 she laid down the principle that not only the royal colonies, but also those with special rights under their charters, should realize that they had obligations to meet, as well as rights to enjoy, the most important of which was their own defense. Under this somewhat rough and ready method of treatment, which was not at all what Burke called it, "salutary neglect," but rather the mercantilist's idea of how a mother country should guide her colonies, the English colonies in America became self-reliant, self-governing, and self-supporting groups, possessed of a spirit of independence and of confidence in their ability to manage their own affairs that made for steady growth and permanence.

During the seventeenth century the government in England retained the character of a medieval personal monarchy, with king and Privy Council still powerful, with the great officers of state still the king's servants, and with the functions of parliament still largely limited to financial and domestic concerns. But in 1689, after the fall of the Stuarts, this form of government underwent a great change. The executive power of king and council steadily declined. The royal office was invaded by the cabinet. The great officers of state were supplanted by small groups of men specially commissioned to perform the duties formerly entrusted to single persons of the king's own appointment. The king's secretaries—his Majesty's principal secretaries of state—became the heads of great executive departments, dispensing patronage and exercising a powerful political influence. The administration of affairs fell, for the most part, into the hands of boards and offices of various sorts, which, though often elaborately organized, were rarely directed by men conspicuous for ability or the gifts of personal leadership. Parliament, particularly the House of Commons, advanced in prestige and importance, enlarging the scope of its activities, gaining in solidarity and self-consciousness, and eventually placing in the hands of officials whose duties were defined by statute, many functions hitherto exercised by the executive. By the middle of the century parliament was settling by legislative enactment many matters that had formerly been determined by executive order only.

Thus, both in England and the colonies, during the period after 1689, powers were shifting and uncertain. In America, the new British system of control made its way slowly and gradually and in the face of determined resistance from private governments that had managed themselves under their charters for many years practically unmolested. It is not surprising that the new British customs officials, whose jurisdictions covered the proprietary and corporate colonies as well as those that were royal, should have met with many discouragements, and have been looked upon as meddlers and busybodies. They in their turn were vocal in their comments on the treatment they received. Even when the system seemed fairly well established, the authority of the royal governors, as expressed in their instructions from the crown, the operations of the vice-admiralty courts and customs officials, and the commercial restrictions—notably those imposed by the Molasses Act of 1733—were subject to dispute, and, at times, to evasion and complete nullification. Such opposition was no part of a deliberate purpose on the part of the colonists; it was inherent in the process of adjustment to a new relationship which was forced upon them and in which they found much that seemed ill adapted to the conditions of growing communities. British rulings often showed complete ignorance of colonial business methods and of colonial conditions generally, and attempts to enforce these rulings, particularly after 1763, disclosed, as never before, the difficulties of applying the British system as defined by the revenue and navigation laws. The royal instructions, in many of their parts, were frequently mere repetitions of earlier drafts; and though old clauses were modified or new ones introduced to meet special situations, the results were rarely very successful. Few attempts seem ever to have been made to adapt the instructions to the actual circumstances of the colonies, and the colonists sometimes thought, as was said in a controversy over a governor's instruction in New York, that the king would never have so instructed his governor had he known the effect of such an instruction on the welfare of the province.

In England the situation was even worse. Men did not know where to look for the sources of authority. They could not determine exactly the functions and powers of the various commissions, boards, and departments that made up the British executive and administrative systems. They were often in doubt as to where the lines should be drawn between the king's authority—which was warranted under the common law but liable to curtailment by statute —and that of parliament, which was established in part by legislative encroachment and in part by a widespread popular conviction that an act of parliament was more likely to be effective than a royal decree. For the colonists, this aspect of the case was complicated by the fact that the royal prerogative remained authoritative in America long after it had ceased to be operative in the government at home; and by the further fact that, at the same time, parliament opposed the authority of the crown even in matters strictly colonial, because it was determined to prevent any extension of the royal power anywhere. Thomas Pownall thought that the colonies ought to be grateful to parliament rather than opposed to it, because on sundry occasions, some of which we have seen, the jealousy of that body for its own rights had saved them from greater subjection to the prerogative of the crown. It is well known that the Board of Trade and parliament did not always agree as to their purposes, and that the colonists were uncertain at times whether to appeal to parliament or the king. Even in respect of the executive itself, those interested in trade and plantations did not know where to make their applications —whether to the Privy Council, the secretary of state, or the Board of Trade. Though among the best informed it was understood that the proper approach to the king was through the Privy Council—by whom matters would be referred to committee and thence to the Board of Trade, the Treasury, the Admiralty, or elsewhere—the procedure seemed so complicated as to deter many from making any application at all. No wonder, then, that appeals of this kind from the colonies to the king were considered, as a rule, a very formidable business.

The result of such executive, administrative, and legislative confusion was inevitably a divided control in matters of great importance, a rivalry of officials, and a looseness of organization that prevented certainty and rapidity of action and sometimes prevented any action at all. It led to a multiplication of offices, widely scattered over the cities of Westminster and London, which hampered coördination of effort and rendered impossible any efficient system of centralized authority. When we add to these defects a low order of political and financial morality, a dearth of leaders possessing statesmanlike qualities, a monopoly of offices by the leading Whig families, an undeveloped sense of responsibility in the performance of public duty, and a failure on the part of the government to comprehend the necessity of new and powerful machinery for the administration of the colonies, we can understand, in part at least, why British colonial management was so inadequate, and why British critics became despondent and extolled the government of France as superior to their own. Evelyn was confronted by many "triste and melancholly moments which the prospect and face of things" forced upon him, and wondered whether the state of politics and public morality might not be the precursor of those last and worst of times which the New Testament foretold as coming upon the world in the days before the final judgment.

In fact, the period from 1713 to 1763 was one of transition, always disturbing to men's minds. By increasing her colonies and strengthening her control, Great Britain gradually widened her horizon and attained a status that was imperial in form. Changes took place also in popular thought and terminology. True the word "empire" had been frequently used by pamphleteers and letter writers as early as 1685, when "R. B." employed it in his little volume, *The English Empire in America,* but with no other meaning than that implied by Raleigh, when a century before he wrote of "rule and empery," or by Thomas Pownall, in his *Principles of Polity, being the Grounds and Reasons of Civil Empire,* published in 1752, wherein he speaks of the "empire of government," "imperium, the power of government," and the "empire of the State." However, in the first half of the eighteenth century it was beginning to connote something more specific than "rule" and "power," and it was used to describe the self-sufficient empire of the mercantilists, the empire of the seas, "that dominion which nature designed us," the maritime empire of the elder Pitt. It can hardly have meant to the men of the early eighteenth century what Milton saw in his prophetic vision, that is, England "with all her daughter lands about her"—a great oceanic, imperial state, a mother land presiding over subordinate communities subject to the will and authority of king and parliament. It may well be doubted if there were many, even among the leaders themselves, who foresaw the imperial form that the greater Britain was to take after her long and successful struggle with France for colonial and commercial supremacy. Such a conception of empire was only vaguely, if at all, a part of the common consciousness until after 1763.

To aid in her struggle for supremacy England needed

all the help the colonists could furnish, not only in the form of direct contributions, but even more in the indirect advantages that they might offer as sources of supply and revenue. The rule that each colony should be self-supporting and bear the burden of its own maintenance was fundamental to the mind of the mercantilist, whose system of public economy was at that time in the ascendant; and, except for the expenses of naval and military protection in all the colonies, and the charges for a part of the administration of Nova Scotia and Georgia, this rule was, at the cost of considerable trouble, consistently adhered to. Unlike the colonies of France, those of Great Britain before 1763 imposed upon the mother country but a slight and constantly diminishing financial obligation—an advantage that was not trifling to a heavily burdened exchequer. More positively advantageous were the contributions that the colonies made of men and material in times of war on colonial soil. Between 1689 and 1763 Great Britain was engaged in four wars with France, each of which was fought in part in America with the coöperation of the colonists, and one with Spain, to which the Northern and Southern colonies contributed a considerable number of men. This military aid was not always as timely or as enthusiastically rendered as it might have been, and sometimes was prompted by motives of self-interest quite as much as by a desire to help the mother country in her hour of need. But even so, of great material benefit to Great Britain was the assistance given by colonial troops on such occasions as the defense of Jamaica in 1703; the attempted expeditions against Canada in 1709 and 1711; the capture of Port Royal in 1710; the Cartagena expedition of 1740;

the capture of Louisbourg in 1745; and the French and Indian War from 1756 to 1763. Both Governor Shirley and Sir William Pepperrell were appointed colonels on the British establishment, with authority to raise regiments of regulars to be paid out of appropriations made by parliament. In the French and Indian War the New England colonies, New York, New Jersey, and Virginia, strained their resources to furnish men and supplies, and in return received from parliament grants of money which eventually reached a total of a million pounds sterling, to recompense them for their outlay and their losses. More or less frequently all the colonies were engaged in wars for local defense, either with the Spaniards in Florida, as was the case with South Carolina; with the Indians on the frontier, as was true at one time or another with nearly all the colonies; or with the Caribs and negroes in the West Indies, a constant danger, particularly in Jamaica.

Though military aid was one of the most conspicuous of the direct benefits accruing to Great Britain from America in the struggle with France, it was scarcely more important than the share which the colonists had in outfitting the British navy. Hundreds of masts, knees, bowsprits, and yards—spruce and pine—were sent over from the forests of New England, New York, and Pennsylvania. Thousands of feet of good oak lumber—white and red—were furnished for naval use, either in England or America; and large quantities of naval stores—pitch, tar, rosin, and hemp—were shipped, partly from New England but in even greater measure from North and South Carolina. Hundreds of vessels built in colonial shipyards were used in England, though rather in the merchant marine than in the royal navy; and many men, born in the colonies and trained in the coastwise service or the fisheries of New-foundland, Nova Scotia, and New England, were to be found on British men-of-war, some volunteers, others impressed from colonial vessels lying in British outports or colonial harbors, for the service of the royal navy. Great Britain's ability to procure from the colonies naval stores and potashes did not save her much actual money, because of the bounties and the high freight rates, but it relieved her somewhat from dependence on Russia and the Scandinavian kingdoms, with whom her balance of trade was always unfavorable, because two-thirds of the payment had to be made in money and only one-third could be made in goods. The building of ships and the training of seamen contributed, as far as they went, to the material resources of a state, the wealth and security of which (as Edward Randolph wrote in 1696) "depended on its trade and navigation." He goes on to say that "the materials for building ships have to be secured from neighboring countries at increasingly heavy rates, liable in time of war, when specially needed, to be cut off entirely. Thus in peace England [is] drained of large sums annually and in war threatened with entire loss of supply." We may not wonder, therefore, that for more than seventy-five years, up to the very eve of the Revolution, naval authorities in England sought material in America for the building and equipping of their ships.

But of greatest value in the eyes of Englishmen, both statesmen and merchants, were the indirect benefits that the colonies conferred, the most profitable of which was colonial trade. England, influenced by the economic views of the time, deliberately discouraged importations from

Background of the Revolution

France, "the dangerous and inveterate enemy of Great Britain," and rejected a French trade which, had it been reciprocally pursued, would have permitted a turnover of business capital many times a year. In its place she cultivated, and greatly overvalued, the trade of her own colonies, where the returns from invested capital could not be assured within less than from one to four years. This commercial war with France, which began with an act of parliament in 1678 and lasted until the Eden treaty of 1786, was started by an English embargo on all French wine, vinegar, brandy, linen, cloth, silk, salt, and paper, and on all manufactures that contained any thread, wool, hair, gold, silver, or leather. In 1688 another act prohibited all commerce with France whatsoever, on the ground that such commerce had "much exhausted the treasure of this nation, lessened the value of the native commodities and manufactures and greatly impoverished the English artificers and handicrafts, and caused great detriment to this kingdom in general." France retaliated, particularly after the outbreak of the Spanish War in 1701, and in the later readjustments duties, estimated by Adam Smith at seventy-five per cent of their value—an amount equivalent to absolute prohibition—were imposed by England on French goods and maintained until 1786. Though the official balance was probably in England's favor, the total trade was inconsiderable, and smuggling increased so enormously that the illicit importations exceeded those that were regularly entered. The policy was damaging for both countries; but the fact that of the two France suffered the more, made it possible for England to profit from her colonial trade.

Mother Country and its Policy

But to England the trade with the colonies appeared in the light of a God-given substitute for the trade of France, for her commercial attitude toward the colonies was determined less by actual economic conditions than by the prevailing ideas about these conditions. English mercantilists maintained that the colonies were not "a burthen but the greatest blessing that Heaven has bestowed upon us; that blessing which in the space of a couple of centuries has multiplied our people, augmented our wealth, and increased our power almost beyond the reach of calculation." In that trade, they said, lay "the basis of Great Britain's strength and power, without which she could not be safe." Furthermore they considered the navigation acts, by which that trade was secured to Great Britain, the "guardian of British prosperity," a "most glorious bulwark, the best acts that ever passed for the benefits of trade." Other mercantilists declared that without these acts the French and Dutch would supply colonial wants and receive the produce of the British colonies in America, "the cornucopia of Britain's wealth"; and they all agreed that to allow the colonies to suffer from inadequate defense or to seek their own advantage by an open trade with Great Britain's rivals would be on her part an act of the greatest folly. It was inevitable, therefore, that Great Britain should build up her system of colonial control on the widely accepted principle that colonies were desirable only as far as they were useful to the states from which they took their origin, and were useful only as far as they procured for those states new advantages and solid means of extending their commerce. But she did not exploit her colonies as France did hers, for the latter made little effort, by means of bounties on colonial materials, by the granting of a monopoly of the home market to colonial staples, and by the admission of colonial ships to the advantages enjoyed by those of the mother country, to favor the colonies, as Great Britain was wont to do, and so to render the colonial relationship as far as possible mutually advantageous.

Thus during the earlier part of the colonial period, at least until the middle of the eighteenth century, Great Britain valued the plantations not as aggregations of people only or as accretions of territory to be used as homes for an overflowing population from England; for the mercantilists held that a territory larger than could be adequately settled or defended, or economically maintained, was a liability not an asset, a burden not a benefit. Rather did she expect them to produce those raw materials that would contribute directly or indirectly to the success of the mother state in its contest with other nations for the supremacy of the seas and for leadership in the commercial and colonial worlds. William Penn interpreted the general view when he said, as far back as 1701, that it was "trade which must make America valuable to England"; and Dummer in his *Defence of the New England Charters*, first printed in 1721, emphasized the point, with even less reservation, when he declared that "the benefit which Great Britain receives from her plantations arises from their commerce." Both these men based their arguments against undue interference with America, as did the British and colonial merchants of a later day, upon the ground of commercial profit. And these arguments were always effective, for, in the opinion of the contemporary Englishmen, all other advantages sank into relative insignificance beside this superlative one, which alone, they believed, justified the existence of colonies.

Therefore when rating the colonies as British assets, Great Britain valued New England and the Middle Colonies much lower than the Southern and West Indian colonies, not only because the former furnished little that could not be as well supplied by Ireland and even by England herself, but also because they had an almost complete monopoly of the provision trade with the tobacco and sugar plantations in America. Then, too, New England furnished the Newfoundland fishermen with provisions, shoes, hose, soap, nets, and lines at a cheaper rate than England herself could supply them, and at the end of the fishing season carried away many fishermen who would otherwise have gone back to England for service in the royal navy. Also, she challenged England's supremacy in the fish markets of Europe by means of the fish caught in her own waters. Thus, in a sense, all the Northern colonies were competitors and commercial rivals of England herself, and through the colonial era British merchants are found complaining of the conflicting purposes of the Briton and the Northern colonist. They declared that should the New Englanders be allowed to cultivate the same products and have liberty to carry them to the same markets, they would certainly destroy the commerce and culture of Great Britain by selling at a lower price. An Exeter merchant, writing in 1751, said that traders of the Northern colonies had all the West India business to themselves and that Britishers could hope for no encouragement "for mixing with them in the commodities of provisions and lumber," for they had things better than the British merchant and could "go to market cheaper." "I am greatly distressed," he adds, "about outward freights for my ships and wish there were encouragement for sending two yearly to the colonies for lumber cargoes, but the traders there are so much nearer to the Sugar Islands and have so many other advantages that an Englishman can neither buy nor sell with them." Later, the Northern colonies were looked upon more favorably as offering a market for British manufactures, but in the early part of the period their competition with England in the West India trade, shipbuilding, and the fisheries, their attitude of political and commercial independence, and their disregard of the interests of the larger commercial world of which they were a part seemed rather to hinder than to advance the common welfare. The most useful colonies to the mother country were the British West Indies with their sugar, and the Southern colonies with their tobacco, rice, indigo, and naval stores; and in order that these commodities should redound to the advantage of Great Britain rather than to that of her rivals, certain staples, such as sugar, tobacco, cotton, and dyewoods had been "enumerated" as far back as 1660, that is, they could be shipped, in vessels British built, owned, and manned, to England only. Later, as other products gained value in British eyes, the list was very considerably extended.

Now, as the colonies increased in number; as colonial trade became more varied, complex, and profitable; and as the menace of French commercial aggression aroused in England a greater interest in the plantations overseas, these ideas regarding the colonies were elaborated and given more articulate and coherent form. British policy became colonial as well as commercial in character—colonial, that is, as far as Great Britain ever had a colonial policy, properly so called, before the nineteenth century. The doctrine of "the self-sufficing empire"—a well turned phrase but one never used contemporaneously—describes a policy which the mercantilists of the period before the Revolution used to support both argument and action. According to this doctrine, the mother country, the sugar and tobacco colonies, the provision or bread colonies, the fisheries, and Africa formed a single economic and commercial whole, made up of mutually sustaining parts, each of which contributed something to the strength and profit of the entire group. The mother country consisted of England, Wales, and the town of Berwick-upon-Tweed, and, after 1707, of Scotland, with Ireland barred from the plantation trade, except in provisions, horses, servants, and linen. The sugar and tobacco colonies included Barbadoes, Jamaica, and the Leeward Islands, which produced sugar, molasses, rum, ginger, pepper, cotton, and dyewoods; and Maryland, Virginia, and the Carolinas, which contributed tobacco, rice, indigo, naval stores, and furs. The provision or bread colonies were Pennsylvania, New York, and New England, the leading staples of which were wheat, flour, bread, and livestock. The fisheries consisted of the waters of Newfoundland and Nova Scotia, where fishing as a source of wealth was cultivated to the almost complete neglect of the land settlements in that part of the British world. By Africa, the fifth part, was meant the western coast from Senegambia to Angola, which furnished the yearly quota of not less than 27,000 negroes, who cultivated the cane, tobacco, and rice fields of the tropical and semi-tropical colonies, where white labor proved wholly inadequate to meet the hard conditions that plantation life imposed.

The mercantilists valued the Northern or bread colonies because they could supply the sugar, tobacco, and rice colonies with bread, flour, meats, fruits, vegetables, houses, horses, sheep, pigs, pipe-staves, headings, and lumber that the latter could not sufficiently produce for themselves. The Southern colonies, also, provided some of these things, and the West Indies raised for the maintenance of their negroes, to a larger extent than is commonly supposed, what were locally known as "ground provisions," thereby often lessening the demand for outside bread and flour, and driving the captains and supercargoes from the bread colonies to seek markets elsewhere, particularly among the French, Dutch, and Spanish islands. But the British West India planters made no effort to supply all that was needed for the upkeep of their tables, houses, and plantations, and consequently the Northern colonies found in the islands of the Caribbean their most lucrative market. As early as 1709 the Board of Trade could report that the British islands in the West Indies would "not be able to carry on their trade, or even to subsist (especially in time of war) without the necessary supplies from the Northern plantations of bread, drink, fish, and flesh of cattle and horses for cultivating their plantations, of lumber and staves for casks for their sugar, rum, and molasses, and of timber for building their houses and sugar works." That the arrangement was satisfactory from the British point of view appears from the remark of a contemporary pamphleteer that "our sugar colonies could hardly subsist without the assistance of those on the continent, and those upon the continent thrive and grow rich by this commerce with our sugar islands, but it is Great Britain that reaps the benefit of both, for all their gains centre here." Thus the New England and Middle colonies, though considered by the mercantilists a detriment rather than a benefit to Great Britain, found themselves necessary though subordinate factors in the general commercial scheme.

During the first half of the eighteenth century, the sugar and tobacco colonies played their part in this "self-sufficing empire" as exporters to Great Britain of their leading staples; while the bread colonies, though sending to the mother country a few products, such as naval stores, furs, flaxseed, whale oil, and—when Great Britain allowed it—grain, corn, and salted provisions, served as secondary and contributory factors, chiefly useful because of the bread and provisions they sent to the Southern and West Indian colonies. France was valuing her colonies in precisely the same way, but without the heavy customs dues and the restrictive features—such as the "enumeration" and the requirement to import manufactured articles through the home ports; and because she had no bread and provision colonies—for neither Canada nor Louisiana could match the British Northern colonies in this respect —she offered a tempting opportunity to the merchants and sea captains of Pennsylvania, New York, and New England to carry their surplus products to her West Indian islands and so to break through the restraints of the British mercantile system. The frequent glutting of the British West Indies with Northern goods which resulted in a dull market; the high prices of return freights of rum, sugar, and molasses; the scarcity of money and bills of exchange which rendered payment of debts uncertain; and the frequent complaints of the inferior quality of the colonial staples—all these things drove the Northern colonies, in the interest of their own prosperity, to find a market where they could. But because this trade between the British Northern colonies and the French and other foreign colonies in the West Indies was contrary to mercantilist principles and to the ends sought in the self-sufficing empire, Englishmen, both at home and in the West Indies, became alarmed. They declared that British subjects in North America were serving themselves with foreign sugar, rum, and molasses, and by so doing not only were transferring to foreigners the benefits of a trade that in its original channel belonged to Great Britain, but also were enriching the foreign sugar colonies and impoverishing their own.

To stop this traffic the well known Molasses Act was passed in 1733, a futile measure, which at best profited no one and was systematically evaded. The New Englanders in particular had to break the act in order to live, for unless they could find some other staples suitable for export to Great Britain than those that lay naturally at hand—and they honestly though without any great enthusiasm tried to find such—they had nothing but the unthinkable alternative of remaining, commercially speaking, in a state of arrested development. The act failed of its purpose because the Northern colonies, which earlier in the century had no more surplus than was sufficient to supply the British islands, were growing so rapidly in population and producing such a surplus of commodities that they became wholly discontented with the narrow and subordinate place assigned them by the mercantilist scheme, and evaded the law in somewhat the mood of the smuggler, who though punished legally was not convinced that he had been punished justly. Unfortunately for the relationship between Great Britain and her colonies British statesmen and merchants of the eighteenth century continued for many years to persist in their efforts to enforce the Molasses Act, as is seen in the many renewals of it that followed its expiration in 1738; but until the enlargement of the act into the Sugar Act of 1764 these efforts were fruitless. In fact, neither Great Britain nor France ever attained or could have attained to that condition of commercial equilibrium which the mercantilist desired, for the theory did not allow for the natural growth in population and resourcefulness of the colonies themselves, nor did it take into account the fact that the time would come when the Northern colonies would demand, in some measure, an independent commercial life of their own.

Mercantilism was essentially a nationalistic policy, selfish as all nationalistic policies are selfish. It fomented war in provoking an economic struggle among the commercial and industrial nations for place, power, and wealth, and sacrificed the welfare of the outlying and dependent parts of a state in the interest of the dominant portion. The British mercantilist wished to shape governmental activity to material ends and to subordinate art and science, culture and intellect, to the gains of trade and commerce. He had as his object the material upbuilding of the state, the increase of its strength, and the improvement of its physical well being. He wanted a monopoly of trade for the realm, as defined by the phrase "England, Wales, and Berwick-upon-Tweed"; and would exclude from the privileges of this monopoly, except as far as they might profit from its indirect advantages, the lesser dependencies, Ireland, Scotland (until 1707), and the colonies, all of which must supplement, not compete with, the mother state. Such monopoly was the basic element of mercantilism, the keystone of its success, and the buttress of its stability. To have colonies that were not coöperative was to weaken and finally to destroy the state itself. To give them an independent life was to counteract all the advantages that arose from the colonial relationship. In the days before the Revolution many of the mercantilists believed that the colonies were "using" the British merchants to further their own ends and resented this breach of the colonial obligation.

Historically considered, mercantilism was the materialistic, self-protective philosophy of a growing state that was striving to win for itself a place of superiority among the nations. It was a doctrine of exclusiveness and self-sufficiency, opposed to cosmopolitan coöperation and to any form of international control. It has its counterpart in the American nationalistic and self-protective policy of the nineteenth and twentieth centuries, the chief characteristics of which are isolation, high protective tariffs, and the subordination of dependencies with their miscellany of governors, some indifferent, others worse, appointed by the president of the United States with the advice of party leaders. There is a great deal of mercantilism left in the world to-day and, owing to the current exaggeration of national and racial differences, the present tendencies in the world seem more mercantilist than ever. Many American nationals still consider foreigners as potential enemies and look upon commerce with them as a form of warfare.

Mother Country and its Policy

They welcome figures which show an excess of exports over imports as marking prosperity, and where the movement is in the other direction, they consider a recovery as an "improvement" in our trade balances. There are still among us many modern mercantilists who believe that government should be conducted by and in the interest of the "captains of industry" and that "success" is still nothing more than the accumulation of wealth. Just as many writers of to-day condemn the mercantilism of the past as injurious and unjust, so in all probability critics of a later century, when it is to be hoped that antagonistic and competing commercial policies may have given way to a more enlightened doctrine of mutual understanding and association among the nations, will censure the commercialism and provincial views of business and government that prevail in the world to-day.

To many the eighteenth century principle of commercial warfare may seem fundamentally wrong, despite the fact that it is in part still in vogue among us; but there can be no doubt that British policy, based on this doctrine of colonial dependence and a prohibitory tariff against France, was eminently successful, in the same way that a similar selfish policy is equally successful among ourselves. In the first place, it gained for Great Britain a position of commanding leadership and commercial supremacy in the world of sea-power and the colonies, and that, too, long before the battle of Trafalgar was fought and won. When in later years, 1792-1793, France for the first time considered the possibility of passing a navigation act of the British type, that is, of the type of the Commonwealth Act of 1651, the revolutionary leaders (the Jacobins) made it abundantly evident that the purpose of such an act was to challenge Great Britain's supremacy in commerce. Advocates of the act, which was finally passed on September 21, 1793, believed, and rightly, that Great Britain owed her maritime success to the commercial policy which she had pursued for a century and a half, and that in order to break her power on the sea it would be necessary to adopt a similar policy. Napoleon, taking over from them the main features of his commercial and colonial programme, retained the act and enforced its provisions as long as there was any hope of competing with Great Britain in the colonial and commercial field. With this hope dashed by the battle of Trafalgar, he was forced to employ other tactics and turned to the blockade system of barring British goods from the European Continent inaugurated by the Berlin Decree of 1806. Thus French policy itself stands as an unimpeachable witness to the effectiveness of the old British colonial system. Whether Great Britain could have attained to her supremacy at sea without adopting enmity against France as a part of her governmental policy is not a matter for us to consider here, but certain is it that the colonies could not have won the War of American Independence without French aid—and to this extent the hatred of France for England at this time contributed to the disruption of Great Britain's colonial empire. If, many Englishmen have believed and still believe, the war and its results were a blessing in disguise, because it saved Great Britain from being engulfed in a cosmopolitan commonwealth, such as the United States is to-day—an issue foreseen one hundred and fifty years ago by Adam Smith and Dean Tucker in England and by William Hooper in

Mother Country and its Policy

America—then the mercantile policy of the eighteenth century, upon the results of which rests the Great Britain of the present time, finds ample justification in history. If mercantilism of the eighteenth century is to have a fair hearing it must be judged not solely from the American point of view or in the light of what we conceive to be the more rational standards of the nineteenth and twentieth centuries.

In other respects than those already enumerated Great Britain profited by her policy. The early dreams of a tropical West taking the place of a tropical East were in part realized. Chocolate, coffee, oranges, lemons, tamarinds, pepper, ginger, and other non-English products were obtained in varying quantities, sometimes as regular shipments from the colonies and sometimes as gifts transmitted by the colonists, both continental and insular, to their friends at home. The trade in dyewoods—fustic, braziletto, and logwood—and in hard woods—mahogany, lignum vitæ, walnut-tree, and oak—attained considerable proportions and was a very important asset to the textile industry and to cabinetmaking in the eighteenth century. The proceeds from the American whale fishery supplemented those from Greenland and the farther north, and whale fins, whale oil, spermaceti candles, and the like were regularly shipped to Great Britain. Hundreds of thousands of furs, skins, and pelts—bear, fox, deer, wildcat, otter, martin, fisher, mink, muskrat, beaver, wolf, raccoon, moose, elk, and buffalo—were sent from nearly every continental colony, notably from New York and South Carolina and the stations of the Hudson's Bay Company; potash, pearlash, and saltpetre, usually imported from the East Indies, were obtained in varying quantities; and after 1750 indigo, chiefly from South Carolina but in some measure from Virginia and North Carolina also, furnished England with a dyeing material usually purchased in Guatemala and Santo Domingo. Before the end of the colonial era, the colonists were exporting to Great Britain, in large amounts, the lesser staple products that as a rule were bought for cash of foreign countries, and in so doing were not only helping Great Britain's balance of trade where it was most unfavorable—as in the East Indies, Russia, and the northern kingdoms of Sweden and Norway—but also saving much good coin to the realm.

Of all the staples that Great Britain obtained from America by far the most important were sugar and tobacco. To British administrators and traders these were the leading commodities, and so valuable were they and so prominent a place did they hold in the esteem of the mercantilists that their influence in shaping British policy toward the colonies was probably greater than even that of politics, war, and religion. They brought increased business to the shippers, freight carriers, and insurance writers of the time, and they made large profits not only for planter and merchant in America, but also for every wholesale and retail dealer, manufacturer, and sugar refiner in England. The merchants and capitalists of the eighteenth century considered these two commodities so much the mainstays of British prosperity that they constantly appealed to the Board of Trade, the Privy Council, and parliament for favorable action in their own behalf and almost invariably succeeded in having their complaints heeded and their petitions met. The British government as well as the British merchants rated these commodities as assets of tremendous consequence, because the duties received from them bulked largest in the customs returns of London and the outports, and so contributed to swell enormously the sum total of the British customs receipts.

From the beginning the colonies lay outside the barriers of the British fiscal system and were obliged to pay heavy duties in England on their own exports, in addition to whatever similar duties they chose to levy on the same commodities at their own customs houses in America. A planter in Barbadoes and the Leeward Islands had to pay the four and a half per cent export duty on sugar and other "dead commodities" at the time of their shipment from the West Indies, and another considerable duty on the arrival of the commodity at London or one of the outports. He might have to pay also the "plantation duty" imposed by the act of 1673, in case he wished to carry his "enumerated" commodity to another plantation. A planter in Virginia or Maryland had to pay a two shilling a hogshead export duty in the colony and an import duty in England, and he might be liable also for the "plantation duty" of a penny a pound on tobacco. Many illustrations could be given of the exceedingly heavy duties actually levied on colonial exports at the port of London, amounting after 1750 to more than sixty per cent of their selling value. For instance, one lot of tobacco worth £1062 paid duties amounting to £625; another worth £1111 paid £759, the proportion varying with the time, the rate, and the price of tobacco. The colonists often protested against these heavy payments, which, with the additional freight, port dues, and commission charges, materially cut down their profits; but so crude were the ideas prevailing in England regarding the shifting and incidence of taxation, that the British government, with the blindness of governments in general, never seemed to grasp the effect the payment of these duties had on the temper of the colonists or to look beyond the immediate importance of the revenue received to the ultimate effect of the duties on producer and consumer.

During the first half of the colonial period the colonies sparsely settled and poor had been valued chiefly as a source of supply for raw materials, but as they increased in population and wealth they began to attract attention as a profitable market for British manufactures and for foreign commodities shipped through British ports. This idea, which had evolved early, attained maturity only toward the middle of the eighteenth century. The sight of two million people—for such was the British estimate of the population of all the colonies in the year 1750—impressed upon the British merchant the importance of paying more attention to the selling side of his business and of interesting himself in the colonists as a buying public able to consume the goods that Great Britain produced. Hence, as early as 1699, arose the policy of restricting manufactures in the colonies, on the ground that the latter should not have the same economic interests as the mother country and should not be allowed to make the same things that Great Britain was making. As the Board of Trade said, all manufactures "ought to be imported from this kingdom"; to do otherwise, the merchants reasoned, would upset the whole commercial scheme.

Mother Country and its Policy

In the decade preceding the treaty of 1763, this business of exporting to the colonies—particularly the continental colonies—the surplus products of Great Britain increased enormously. Scarcely a vessel left English or Scottish ports—London, Bristol, Liverpool, Hull, or Glasgow—but carried large quantities of goods manufactured in those cities or in the cities of the interior—Manchester, Birmingham, Sheffield, Leeds, and many others—and exported either in response to orders from planters and storekeepers in America, or to be sold on commission in colonial towns or at stores owned by Scottish merchants chiefly at various points along the rivers of Maryland and Virginia. This "American trade" attained very large proportions, rising, according to accepted estimates, from two hundred and fifty thousand pounds a year in 1700 to four million, five hundred and twenty thousand pounds in 1770, and constituting not less than from one-sixth to one-third of the total trade of Great Britain, depending on the year. Before 1750 the colonies exported more than they imported and received cash in return, but after 1755 their imports from Great Britain began to exceed their exports, until the balance in Great Britain's favor amounted to nearly two millions in 1760 and nearly three millions in 1770. Thus the business of exporting manufactured goods to America was advancing by leaps and bounds, and after the failure of the non-importation movement in 1769-1770, British merchants indulged in what has been called "a mad mercantile speculation," in which trade was being built up on capital borrowed in England and Scotland and on a system of long-term credits in America, extended, as Governor Bernard

said, "beyond all bounds of prudence." This inflation of
credit had been carried dangerously far in the years immediately preceding the Revolution, for it seemed unlikely that the colonists could ever pay so huge an indebtedness either in cash or commodities. As early as 1768
a Bristol merchant could write to a correspondent in
America who owed him £11,000, complaining of the "many
inconveniences and distresses" that the latter's "great and
long standing ballance hath for a good while past heaped
upon" him, and adding that his "credit has now come to
such a pass as to admit of no longer delay." As the colonists
had no sufficient surplus of staples with which to pay their
debts and very little gold or silver, they were forced to
meet their obligations as best they could, "through different channels and by a round of commerce," often by way
of Spain, Portugal, the Straits, or the West Indies. For
want of a sufficient medium of exchange they were always
cramped in their trade and were never able to do the business they might have done had England been willing or
able to find a remedy or offer some kind of monetary relief.

Nevertheless, to all outward seeming the colonies throve
and prospered. Their apparent wealth increased, imports
became more varied in kind and luxurious in quality, and
conditions of life and standards of taste, particularly in the
towns and on the large plantations, mounted steadily in the
scale of comfort and elegance and even of extravagance.
Dress, house furnishings, food, and amusements tended
toward elaboration and display and the gratification of personal vanities. The cost of living rose; salaries and fees became insufficient and had to be increased; speculation in
real estate was indulged in by those with capital to invest;

and over-confidence, accompanied by a prodigality of expenditure and an itch for gambling, sometimes resulted in financial embarrassment and even bankruptcy. Much of the prosperity was illusory, for it was based on credit inflation and excessive issues of paper currency. Hard money became exceedingly scarce, and the necessity of meeting colonial indebtedness resulted in a persistent drift of that money toward Great Britain. To many observers, even as early as 1774, a financial crisis in the business world seemed much more imminent than a break with the mother country.

To the people of Great Britain this trade of America seemed even more valuable than it did to the colonies. It certainly aided the growth of the cities of both England and Scotland, stimulated their industrial output by furnishing a market for their surplus manufactures, multiplied their factories, and augmented their resources. It gave employment to large numbers of British as well as colonial ships, encouraged the building of larger vessels, and gave rise to those great mercantile houses in every port of entry and many inland towns that were concerned with the business of handling, in one way or another, the staples and orders of the colonial world. But the very expansion of the trade, conducted as it was on a system of long and precarious credits extended to colonial customers, carried with it serious consequences; and it was not only the value of the trade itself but even more the vast indebtedness involved that led the merchants of England and Scotland to band together in 1766, 1768, and 1775 for the purpose of bringing about the repeal of such injurious legislation as the Stamp Act, the Townshend Act, and the Prohibitory Act. Of their success in these attempts something will be said later.

The state, too, deemed the American trade an asset of the greatest importance and disclosed its mercantilist sympathies in the drafting of treaties and the passage of parliamentary legislation. The eighteenth century was a time of wars and political alliances, owing their origin to the efforts of diplomats to maintain a balance of power in Europe, when a system of public credit had hardly come into existence and when the greatest need of governments was available money in the form of coin or bullion wherewith to meet the expenses of statecraft. Money was wanted for the support of diplomacy, the equipment and upkeep of armies, the hiring of troops, the furnishing of the munitions of war, and the subsidizing of allies. Many of these operations were cash transactions, in which payment was made in gold, silver, and bills of exchange. Whigs and Tories alike believed that for the profit of the state itself the economic dependence of the colonies should be maintained, and although the former relied on industry as the main factor in material prosperity and the latter looked to land as the basis of a sound political life for the community, both parties were opposed to any change in the colonial relationship that would make the colonies less serviceable to the mother country.

There was another side to colonial trade, "a precious commodity," as one merchant called it, "but subject to many casualties." At best it was always uncertain, and those who had a part in it were often anxious and full of foreboding. Some years were notorious for their tedious and irregular returns. The year 1736, for example, was reported as "intollerably bad, sales very slack, and prices much too low for their costs," though why this was so is difficult to discover. In the eighteenth century the British merchant became less and less inclined to receive raw materials, particularly the heavy staples from the Northern colonies which were troublesome to handle and hard to dispose of. He preferred to send over manufactured goods and receive his remittances in money, but coin was always difficult to obtain in America and expensive to ship, and bills of exchange were the usual medium. In some parts of the colonial world such bills, which had to be drawn against accumulated credits in England, were almost impossible to secure and had to be purchased, if at all, at high rates of exchange, from fifty to eighty per cent. Moreover, during the years after 1755, these bills became more and more unreliable and frequently went to protest, because there was no colonial credit in England to meet them; and protests always involved additional expense, delay, and in some cases serious loss. Often and bitterly did the British merchants complain of the failure on the part of the American merchants and planters to settle their accounts, and many a one, who not infrequently was doing business on a very narrow margin himself, was compelled to carry a burden of credit far greater than his own capital would bear while for two, three, and even four years he waited to get his pay for goods he had sent to America. In rapidity of payment the colonies differed greatly, the Northern colonies being much less dependable than the West Indies. In the eighteenth century the West India planters presented a balance against Great Britain, but they spent their cash or their accumulated credits, not in the islands where they made their money, but for houses, lands, and political and social positions in the mother country. The continental colonists,

Background of the Revolution

availing themselves of this practice of the West India planters, were always glad to use their own credits acquired in the West India traffic to obtain there bills of exchange with which to pay their British correspondents. There is no doubt that the difficulty of obtaining bills, the insecurity of payment, and the general scarcity of money in the colonies were serious drawbacks to trade and one often wonders that Englishmen and Scotsmen were willing to continue risking their capital at ventures so precarious in character. So closely were the two countries knit financially and commercially that a period of depression in the colonies affected the merchant and manufacturer in England and Scotland; while a business failure in London or elsewhere was always felt by the customers of the unfortunate firm in America. Hazards of trade touched Briton and colonial alike.

To the colonist the trade was always more or less of a gamble. What he wanted was a good market and a quick return; what he frequently got was a poor market, where sales were slow, debts difficult to collect, and bills of exchange impossible to obtain; where either there was no return at all or where a return was secured but at so high a price as to leave no profit. Yet even an unsatisfactory freight was better than a return empty or in ballast, for to come back "dead freighted" was usually accounted a disaster. It was this need of a profitable return that led many ship captains, who arrived early at a British West India market and sold promptly, to go on to the French islands, where the cost of a return freight was frequently lower on account of the favorable climatic and agricultural conditions and the greater cheapness of slave labor. The merchants were always looking for new lines of trade and were always ready to combine in ventures to any colony or port where the outlook was promising. But their staples were not always of the best. That their flour was too tightly packed and musty, coarse, and ill bolted; their tobacco badly prised, of poor quality, mean, black, and sour; their wheat full of weevils; their lumber insufficiently seasoned; their pitch and tar filled with dross and water; their flax-seed light, badly cleaned, and thin-bodied; and their bees-wax dirty in color instead of clear and bright—such were the complaints of which we hear. And these were justified, for the continental colonies were none too particular in the preparation of their products, and in the Northern and Middle colonies there was no inspection system worthy of the name, except perhaps for flour in New York. There was always danger from wind and storm, castaways and wrecks, as well as from unreliable agents, rascally captains and supercargoes, leaky vessels, and tedious passages. In all cases there was great difficulty in getting news of ships, for the carrying of mail by sea captains was a courtesy, not an obligation, and letters were frequently delayed or lost, particularly when sent by private hands. In the passage from the West Indies to London, sugar lost from pilfer-age, wastage, and differences of tare, at a medium, full eight per cent for the clayed variety and about twenty-five per cent for the coarser products; and tobacco, suffering from shrinkage and other causes, was on receipt generally estimated at less than the bills of lading called for. The colonists as well as the British merchant dreaded the ap-proach of war, which raised prices and freight rates and advanced enormously the cost of insurance, the latter being dependent on the element of safety and varying according to the efficiency of convoys, the influence of embargoes, the reports and rumors of captures, and the times and directions of sailing. The insurance rates on ships were always higher during the hurricane months of August and September, and were raised or lowered according to the extent of the convoying, which in war times was furnished by the Admiralty for all the colonies and for Africa and the West Indies in periods of peace on account of piracy and the danger from foreign rivals. Finally, all the merchants had to reckon with a scarcity of sailors, as well as with that perennial menace to peaceful trading relations, an unstable and ever depreciating colonial currency.

Despite all these drawbacks, the trade flourished and was profitable to all, particularly to Great Britain. Whatever might be the various balances of trade existing among the continental American colonies or between the continental colonies and the West Indies—and to have a favorable balance of trade was the object of every colony in its relations with the others—the eventual balance was, after 1755, favorable to Great Britain, at least on paper. The goods that were exported to America from the mother country were more than sufficient to pay for the staples that the colonies furnished; and consequently Great Britain, in her eighteenth century dealings with the colonies, began her career as the creditor nation of the world. But credit without assurance of payment is hazardous and in the long run destructive of confidence. There was scarcely a large merchant or planter or storekeeper below the Pennsylvania-Maryland line who was not in debt to his correspondent in England or Scotland. There are exceptions to this statement, particularly among the merchants of Charleston and

the planters of the West Indies, who were generally able
to meet their trade balances and so to keep out of debt to
England, though not out of debt to the Northern colonies,
whose chief supply of hard money came from their favorable balance of trade with the South and the West Indies.
But taking the American trade as a whole, the exports from
Great Britain far exceeded the imports, and the balance of
cost had to be made up in coin, bills of exchange, or drafts
on the Bank of England. The colonists met their balances
fairly well, despite the great scarcity of hard money, until
1770, when what would seem to have been an orgy of
buying in the colonies and of selling in England sent the
indebtedness up to nearly three millions of pounds, and
ushered in a brief period of extravagance and inflation.
The fall was rapid. By 1774 imports and exports approached an equilibrium, personal credit in England suffered a severe check, and until the passage of the Prohibitory Act, the balance was again in favor of the colonies and
hard money flowed once more from England to America.
But for twenty years the total balance had been in Great
Britain's favor and her statesmen greatly desired that it
should remain so, for such a state of affairs meant a steady
flow of available cash into the kingdom wherewith to aid
in meeting the expenses of state policy. Such a drift of
money made it possible for Great Britain to remain solvent
in the struggle with France during the Seven Years' War,
when that state, under the terrific drain of monarchical expenditure and an unjust distribution of taxation, was passing into that condition of financial bankruptcy which ended
in the French Revolution.

The sum of England's wealth was augmented from

many sources. It was increased not only by the heavy and burdensome customs duties levied on imports and exports, but also by the very considerable sums of money that were spent by the colonists themselves during their visits to the mother country. The number of colonial visitors to England was probably greater than is commonly supposed and the money thus disbursed probably reached a figure that would surprise us if we had the total. Sir Matthew Decker complained that Englishmen did not sufficiently encourage foreigners to travel and spend money in England and thought that Englishmen themselves were too fond of traveling and spending money abroad; but as far as those living in the British colonies were concerned the trend of travel, like that of colonial money, was all in favor of England. Southern planters went over for business or pleasure, carrying letters of introduction that served for social as well as mercantile purposes. Sometimes they sent their sons to be educated at schools near London or to be entered at one or other of the Inns of Court for training as lawyers, and less often they allowed their daughters to cross the water to have a taste of English life and to gain experience and manners in the social surroundings of the metropolis. Invalids sought to recover their health at Bath or Tunbridge Wells or to consult physicians in London or elsewhere. Prospective pharmacists and doctors went to London or Edinburgh for their training as apothecaries or physicians, and prospective merchants learned their business in the countinghouses of leading mercantile firms in London, Bristol, or Glasgow, the heads of which were often personal friends or relatives. All these people, men and women, spent in

England money which they brought with them in cash, letters of credit, or bills of exchange, or which they received from some merchant, who acted as their banker, charging the amount to the debit of their correspondent in America.

Then there were the absentee planters from the West Indies, who, like the nabobs of India, dissipated the profits of their plantations in efforts to obtain political and social preferment and, as is often the case with the *nouveaux riches*, scattered their wealth with a prodigality out of all proportion to the success attained. But they served to counteract whatever disadvantage might occur from the unfavorable balance of trade with the West Indies, for they brought their wealth with them to England and so retained their character as Englishmen, giving to the traffic with the West Indies the nature of an internal rather than a foreign trade. The writer of *Miscellaneous Reflections on the Peace* in 1749 summed up the situation when he wrote, "We might likewise look round and consider the great and rich families settled and established in this island, whose ancestors acquired their fortunes in America; and this would show us two things, first, that very large fortunes are acquired there, and, next, that when so acquired they are laid out here. Now I conceive," he adds, "that let a man come from what country he will, if he brings with him money enough to purchase a large estate, this nation is the gainer by him, just as much as that purchase amounts to; for the land was here before, remains here still, and the money that purchases it into the bargain."

The money, thus expended, which went to swell the sum total of Britain's wealth, was augmented to some extent by the returns, always small and at times quite negligible,

Background of the Revolution

that accrued to the exchequer from various other sources: from the quit-rents paid by large numbers of the colonists on their lands; from the four and a half per cent export duty in Barbadoes and the Leeward Islands—a revenue that ought to have been laid out in the colonies themselves, but was not so spent as a rule; and from the "plantation duty" collected in America by the royal customs officials there, all of which had to be paid in the sterling money of Great Britain or its equivalent. Something was obtained from the fines and forfeitures arising in the royal colonies, from the shares in treasure-trove and pirate captures, from the proportions of prizes of war taken at sea, and from the king's thirds which came from the condemnation of ships seized for illegal trading and tried in the various vice-admiralty courts in the colonies. Small sums also were received from the sale, at four or five pounds apiece, of Mediterranean passes to colonial merchants and ship captains, chiefly, but not exclusively, men of the Northern colonies. That for twenty years after 1755 there was a steady flow of sterling money from nearly every part of the colonial world in the direction of Great Britain, and that British statesmen in fostering colonial trade wished to make this flow continuous and permanent, are facts which played an important part in determining the policy of Great Britain toward her colonies. Without a proper comprehension of these facts colonial history cannot be understood, because British policy was based upon them, and without a knowledge of British policy colonial history becomes a matter of merely American concern, imperfect and incomplete. The profits from colonial trade constituted the chief advantage that Great Britain had in her colonies, and the effects of colonial trade in shaping British policy constituted one of the heaviest grievances of which the colonists complained in estimating the value to themselves of the colonial connection with the mother country.

It was inevitable that members of growing communities with interests of their own—merchants and planters, West Indian as well as continental—should have taken the measure of the British regulations and have determined in a critical spirit the disadvantages that resulted from the commercial restrictions imposed upon them by the mother country. They objected to the heavy duties placed upon their products in England and to the obligation of having to carry their "enumerated" commodities to Great Britain —an obligation that barred them from foreign markets, unless they were willing to sustain the burden and expense of a double voyage involving them in a loss estimated at from thirty to forty per cent for freight, landing, housing, wastage, and the like. They objected to the requirement that they purchase their clothing, hardware, and other necessaries of life from England only, and declared that this limitation upon their range of purchase placed them at the mercy of the merchants and manufacturers of Great Britain, who by means of this monopoly were able to control prices and to compel them to pay higher rates for European and other goods than would have been the case had they bought these goods directly from the foreign markets themselves. They objected also, in cases where they were allowed to take unenumerated staples directly to Europe, to the necessity of going home by way of England in order to make up a return cargo of such manufactured articles as would yield a profit in America, thus increasing their charges and curtailing their choice of goods. They did not like to be compelled always to buy at the "company's store." Just as the English mercantilists, at the beginning of the century, expressed their admiration for the French system of colonial control, so the merchants and planters in America deemed the British regulations far less liberal than those of France, where there were only light duties, no "enumeration," and no restriction upon their field of purchase. Self-interest underlay their criticisms as it underlay the policy of the mercantilists in England. Each group was consulting its own wishes and catering to its own needs, and out of the irrepressible conflict thus provoked arose that century-long activity in smuggling and illicit trade which marked the effort of the colonists to attain commercial freedom and to develop their own independent commercial life. How extensive such smuggling was, in proportion to the whole volume of colonial trade, it is impossible to say, but it went on in some measure wherever an opportunity offered—in Newfoundland, along the Atlantic coast from Maine to Georgia, and notoriously in the West Indies. It was an illegal trade because it was contrary to the acts passed by the English parliament for its regulation; and in the eyes of the mercantilists it was a pernicious trade because it was pursued to the detriment of the mother state, whose interests they believed transcended those of the colonies and should receive preference, no matter what might be the results for the colonies themselves. The latter were expected, as a matter of course, to adjust their interests to those of the composite British group known as the self-sufficing empire.

But in order that the colonies should perform this func-

tion of contributing to the wealth and power of the greater
Britain, of which they were a part and in whose success
they were to share, it was necessary that they recognize the
policy of colonial subordination, and submit themselves to
the unhampered control of the mother country, acknowl-
edging their dependence upon and subjection to her authority, particularly in all that concerned trade and commerce. There could be no arbitration of this relationship or
compromise upon the principle therein involved. Colonies
possessing an independent commercial and economic life
of their own were not wanted in the self-sufficing empire,
because, as far as Englishmen of the age could see, they
could be only a burden without offering any compensating
advantages. The business of those in England concerned
with colonial affairs was to adapt the varying needs and
circumstance of the colonies to the superior rights and
privileges of the mother country and to the prerogatives
of the crown. British officials watched with care to see that
the colonies did nothing to hamper British colonial trade
or discriminate against the activities and interests of those
engaged in it; and parliament passed many laws dealing
with debt, bankruptcy, coinage, and paper currency that
were designed to protect the British merchant doing business with America, sometimes, undoubtedly, at the expense
of the colonists themselves. There are many orders in
Council and many acts of parliament that can be understood only in the light of this policy, which was born not
of British wilfulness or desire to tyrannize or even to med-
dle, but of a conviction, deeply entrenched in the British
mind, that the moment a colony attempted to act solely for
its own benefit and without regard to its proper status as a

dependent and sustaining member of the British oceanic world, it ceased to fulfil the duty incumbent upon it. This conviction, fashioned in the hard school of experience, widely prevailed in the eighteenth century, particularly before 1763, and was maintained the more strictly because of the Britisher's respect for precedent and tradition.

In all other respects, however, the attitude of British statesmen and legislators disclosed a desire to do everything that was possible to promote the well being of the colonies. There was nothing sentimental or altruistic about this attitude, for even the most purblind of British officials must have seen that colonies to be useful should be well protected, prosperous, and in the main contented; nevertheless, it shows that British policy was based on fairly consistent principles and was neither whimsical nor capricious. As long as the colonies did not question her constitutional authority or interfere with the course of trade, as determined by her laws, Great Britain allowed them full freedom of action, aided them in defense, and within certain limits granted to their "enumerated" commodities a monopoly of the British market. In a number of instances —as in the case of silk, indigo, hemp, masts, and naval stores—she stimulated production by a liberal system of bounties, and at all times gave such encouragement as she could to industrial experiments in various directions. She rarely concerned herself with colonial politics or with the routine of colonial administration, and in all matters which she specially reserved for her own supervision, such as the reviewing of colonial legislation, the drafting of governors' commissions and instructions, the settling of intercolonial quarrels and disputes, and the deciding of cases on appeal from colonial courts, she acted, except in a few noteworthy instances, with as much promptness and as much desire for justice as she used in handling similar matters at home. She wanted profitable colonies and was willing to make concessions in order that their vigor and usefulness should not be impaired.

British authorities were generally better in intention than in achievement, for the colonial machinery at Whitehall and in the City of London was never designed for the government of colonies in any modern sense of the word. It had no higher object than the regulation of trade and commerce and the directing of colonial activities in the interest of the mother country. In carrying out even so limited a purpose, Great Britain had to depend on a not very virtuous or very energetic order of human nature, and was hampered by a cumbersome body of customs, conventions, and traditions that constantly interfered to prevent a conscientious performance of duty and a rapid despatch of business. British officials in the colonies were not consistently backed up at home, were often blamed and neglected, and were generally overworked and underpaid, a situation characteristic of British colonial management in later days as well; while British officials in England took little pains to acquaint themselves with conditions in the colonies or even with the geography of the regions they controlled, a state of ignorance that could be illustrated many times over and of which De Foe complained as early as 1704, in connection with official knowledge of the countries of Europe. Furthermore, administration was impeded by politics, discipline was lost in the scramble for office, and merit and ability were rarely considered in appointments

Background of the Revolution

either at home or abroad. Except in a few instances, second-rate men conducted the government of England during these years, while the part that civilians took in the management of the army and navy was characterized not only by incompetence but also by peculation and bribery, often on an enormous scale. Such were the leading features of British colonial policy and conduct down to the year 1763.

III.
Conditions Leading to the Revolt of the Colonies

Conditions Leading to the Revolt
of the Colonies

THE years of American history which inter-vene between the Peace of Paris and the outbreak of the War of Independence have been subjected in the past to an examination so minute as to render seemingly unnecessary any further investigation of the subject. But a careful reconsideration of the evidence in the case shows that in attempting to find an explanation for the events of those years, we have done what no scientist would do in dealing with physical phenomena—devoted our attention to but one set of influences and neglected others that entered in as essential and material parts of the problem. We have viewed these events, not unnaturally and not wrongly, as a part of American history; but we have failed to see that primarily they were but a part of the history of British colonization and should be interpreted in the light, not of the democracy that was to come years later, but of the ideas and practices regarding colonization that were in vogue in Great Britain at the time.

The problems of our early history were British colonial problems first and American problems afterwards, and only when they are treated thus can we hope to solve them. By means of revolution, a people already capable of maintaining a separate existence attained independent statehood, after they had deliberately rejected the principles

Background of the Revolution

underlying that great experiment in colonial expansion which had engaged British statesmen since 1607. A time had come in the course of that experiment when, as it appeared to Englishmen of the day, Great Britain's revenue, the heavy expenses of her wars, and the prosperity of her mercantile and landed classes had become to no small extent dependent on the colonies, that were thought of, not as political communities with highly developed social and economic needs of their own, but as areas of occupied and cultivated land, belonging to Great Britain and designed to serve as of profit to her government and people. Anything that hindered or checked colonial trade tended to injure and even to ruin the business of the merchants and manufacturers in England and Scotland and to force the workmen of the factories out of employment. These views regarding the colonies, as long as they remained colonies, were never absent from British minds.

The year 1763 has always and rightly been considered a great turning point in the history of America's relations with the mother country, and the following features of the relationship emphasize the significance of that momentous year.

First, by her victory over France, Great Britain obtained peace and a securely established imperial status. She had not been consciously or aggressively aiming at empire but had attained it through efforts directed to other ends, the meaning of which at that time neither ministers nor people wholly comprehended and the results of which few of them could have foreseen. Self-interest had been a powerful influence in carrying on the experiment of colonization and business sagacity had governed its course; but finally

Revolt of the Colonies

Great Britain, who had borne a heavy burden of responsibility without any certainty of success, had emerged from a complex of difficulties only to find herself facing the solution of new and troublesome problems, the penalty of her victory. In the past men had spoken of "empire," meaning the self-sufficient empire of the mercantilists rather than a thing of territory, centralization, maintenance, and authority. After 1763, however, territorial empire came into real and visible existence, and writers, both British and colonial, became aware that "imperialism" meant something more than commerce and colonies and that the colonial problem, with which they were familiar only in its mercantile aspects, had taken on a distinctly territorial and political form. They realized that to the regulation of trade and the struggle with other powers for a share of the profits of the earth must now be added the difficult task of territorial administration and support.

Thus a new issue, that of territorial imperialism, emerged to perplex the souls of British statesmen, and so deeply did its significance become ingrained in departmental habits of thought and routine and so little were those in office affected by the American War and its attendant circumstances that imperialistic methods remained dominant in Great Britain long after the Revolutionary War had come to an end. The loss of the American colonies taught Great Britain no lesson regarding her other colonial obligations, except as far as it aroused in her statesmen the determination to avoid in the future any repetition of so fratricidal a struggle. It also made possible the passage by parliament of the constitutional act of 1791 for Canada, which was designed to correct earlier mistakes in colonial government and was destined to become the first constitution, properly so called, of a British colony. Such other colonies as remained to her ceased, officially at least, to be objects of importance and concern. The colonies themselves were no longer self-supporting, as they had been during the period of mercantilist control, and, as no readjustment was made in their machinery of administration, they cost the British taxpayer large sums for maintenance. Mercantilism as a working policy influenced official thought less and less, and the old colonial system, under which the rebellious inhabitants of the thirteen colonies had developed so strong a spirit of independence and self-reliance, was replaced in the remaining colonies by another distinctly autocratic and paternal in character. For many years after the close of the American War, Great Britain's tendency was to employ for her colonies an imperialistic system of administration.

In 1763 the most troublesome and embarrassing problem for imperialism was that of administering the wide-stretching area of largely unoccupied land, stretching westward to the Mississippi and southward to the Gulf of Mexico, which as a result of the treaty of Paris had unexpectedly come into British hands. The mercantilists felt that the surrender of Guadeloupe and the retention of Canada was nothing less than a defeat for their policy. They looked upon Guadeloupe as a profitable island, even though it might become in time a dangerous competitor in the sugar trade, and considered Canada a barren waste, producing, as far as they could see, nothing which was profitable to Great Britain except furs. They maintained that the annexation of so much territory, sparsely occupied or not occupied at all and bound to involve the mother country in heavy expenses for support without commensurate returns in the way of income, was contrary to the principles on which mercantilism was founded. As we see the problem to-day, it is evident that so wide a departure from previous colonial practice and experience was certain to burden the mediocre British statesmanship of the period with a responsibility greater than it could bear.

Secondly, in 1763 Great Britain faced a very different body of colonists from those that had confronted her in the early part of the century. Then they had been comparatively few in number, poor, and unaware of their own strength; but during the fifty years of peace, commercial expansion, and war, following the treaty of Utrecht, they had become wealthy and powerful, and as far as self-government and the ability to manage their own affairs were concerned were quite competent to stand alone. Freed from the ever menacing danger of the French on their borders and competent to receive concessions similar to those which Great Britain was to make to her great self-governing dominions in the nineteenth century, they were now crown colonies only in name and were conducting themselves, in many respects, as autonomous states. In public utterance they expressed "a steady unshaken loyalty, fidelity, and warm devotion" to the king and the house of Hanover (so a Connecticut address phrased it in 1766); but in fact they were fast becoming impatient of too strict an exercise of the royal prerogative and of the claims of a parliament already excessively sensitive regarding its own sovereign power.

Thus after the spring of 1763, when the peace of Paris

Background of the Revolution

was signed and the colonies emerged from the shadow of war, new influences, long in the making, for the first time became active. To the old and well tried colonial policy of mercantilism was now to be added a new and untried policy of imperialism; and the policy resulting from the combination of these antagonistic elements was to be applied to a greatly enlarged colonial area and to a high-spirited body of colonists already freed in many respects from the British connection. But mercantilism and imperialism had nothing in common. Mercantilism, based on the business man's idea of "pay as you go," that is, of promoting commercial undertakings that promised to make money, demanded that no territory be acquired except such as would bring in an adequate return on the investment. Imperialism, on the other hand, which accepted the opening up of new territory in the hope (inevitably long to be deferred) that an expanding population would provide a market for British goods, had no regard for the immediate profits of the mercantilist, and for the purpose of administering the new territory was willing to draw on sources of wealth already developed.

No British mercantilist, with his eye on the balance sheet, would have consented for a moment to the acquisition, merely as a glorious liability, of overseas possessions that had no immediate prospect of becoming self-supporting or profitable to the mother country; and some have supposed that Louisbourg was given back to France in 1748 because in official circles the opinion prevailed that the benefits would not compensate for the expense. No one could think that the western lands in America, ceded by France in 1763, would be able to pay for themselves in many a long year. Yet in the meantime the costs of organization and maintenance had somehow to be met and no man could tell beforehand how this was to be done. In the palmy days of mercantilism, no orthodox mercantilist would have dreamed of raising a revenue in the colonies by legislative enactment in England; nor would he have advocated the use of force or the employment of a policy of coercion. But after 1763 mercantilist ideas became inextricably interwoven with those that were imperial, and the mercantilist group, which had been so powerful in the years before the peace, began to be replaced by many loosely compacted parties of varying shades of opinion. The more conservative continued to view the colonies strictly as commercial assets, whereas others were coming to believe that extent of territory and the exercise of authority were more worthy of consideration by a state of real grandeur, such as Great Britain had now become, than were the mere advantages of traffic. Pitt expressed a growing opinion when he characterized traders and merchants as "Little, paltry, peddling fellows, vendors of two-penny wares and falsehoods, who under the idea of trade sell everything in their power—honour, truth, conscience; who without ever regarding consequences and that general ruin might ensue, press forward to the goal of lucre and cut out the shortest passage to their own interests. Men who act upon the most illiberal principles; children of the world, who have no attachment but to the shrine of Mammon." The policy of weighing events in the scales of the tradesmen selling goods behind the counter was becoming distasteful to many Englishmen of the period, and in this shifting attitude of mind imperialism was to find its most favorable opportunity of growth.

But as events were to prove, in almost every attempt that they made to defray these extra expenses incurred in the administration of the newly acquired provinces overseas, British statesmen affronted in one way or another the colonies in America, because they were thinking in terms, not of the accepted mercantilism but in those of the new imperialism. That the new policy was certain to be expensive appears from the variety and complexity of the problems involved. British statesmen were called upon to deal with the recently acquired lands in such a way as to satisfy the claims of the colonists and to meet fairly the demands of speculators and prospective settlers. They had to furnish adequate supervision of the fur trade and protection for the western Indians, long the prey of unscrupulous traders and restless land-seekers. They had to provide such treatment of the French Roman Catholic inhabitants of Canada in matters of religion, government, and finance, as would align them with the English in the defense of the newly acquired province. They had to decide on some plan of defending this enlarged area, not only against outraged Indian tribes but also against France, who might at any time find a pretext for a renewal of hostilities. And all these new and difficult matters were under the jurisdiction of men who having come into office as representatives of factions were unable to agree among themselves. Furthermore, many of them were incompetent to decide upon any statesmanlike policy and were inclined to let things drift. Even when decisions were reached, as in the Proclamation of 1763, the Quebec Act of 1774, and the various measures regulating Indian affairs and the fisheries, the American radicals put the worst possible construction on the ministerial programme and attributed to the British government aims and motives that probably never entered a British mind. The fact that the colonists over and over again declared that they had no intention of objecting to any act of parliament relative to trade and asked only for a return to conditions as they existed before the Sugar Act of 1764 shows that imperialism and not mercantilism was the first cause of the eventual rupture, and demonstrates further that the "ruinous system of colony administration," as the first Continental Congress called it, which was inaugurated after 1763, was not due to the principles or methods of the old British colonial policy, as writers on colonial history have long maintained.

Of all the obligations of the imperial policy that which concerned finance proved in the end to be the rock upon which the British system foundered. The exchequer at home was already strained by a huge deficit that burdened the domestic taxpayer to an extent unknown to the overseas subjects of the crown. Even if a comprehensive and practicable solution of all the difficulties could be found, which at best was unlikely, the additional outlay of money required could scarcely be secured without subjecting British subjects—particularly the landowning classes, which looked with ill favor upon any increase in the land tax—to a weight of taxation out of all proportion to the advantages likely to accrue to the realm as a whole. The landowners and the merchants were not in accord on this point, for the former wanted a reduction of the land tax and an increase of the duties on sugar and tobacco; while the latter

Background of the Revolution

argued for an increase of the land tax and a relief from the heavy customs dues. In 1744 a mercantilist writer had expressed the views of his class when he said: "Let us earnestly cultivate the known branches of trade, be ready to revive the old and industriously to strike out new. Let us willingly submit to the heaviest taxes at home, rather than load our plantations, from whence we draw the greatest part of our wealth, which enables us to pay [these taxes . . . and so] to secure to us that dominion which nature designed us, the Empire of the Seas." But twenty years later, under the financial conditions following a long and expensive war, this view of the case carried little weight with a parliament made up largely of representatives of the landowning class. These men believed that the colonists rather than the mother country profited both from the opening of the western lands and from such measures of defense as might be taken to guard their western frontiers, and that therefore they should bear a part of the new financial burden, relieving the mother country of taxes that before the war British subjects might have been better able to bear. The failure in the colonies of the system of voluntary quotas during the war rendered wholly problematical the part that the colonists were likely to take of their own accord in aiding Great Britain on the financial side. The question at stake, therefore, was how to obtain the financial coöperation of America without wounding colonial susceptibilities and arousing fears of British coercion.

The first experiment was made in the old field of mercantilism, that is, of colonial trade. The navigation acts, particularly the Molasses Act of 1733, had been evaded by the colonists, whenever their interests demanded it and the conditions were favorable; and during the war with France their intercourse with the enemy had reached such a height that even the more honorable of the colonists themselves had condemned it as almost equivalent to an act of treason. The British exchequer had received very little direct revenue from America, and, as the Board of Trade frankly acknowledged, the customs receipts from the "plantation duty" were not sufficient to defray one-fourth of the cost of collection, being often reduced to the vanishing point by neglect, connivance, and fraud. Partly, therefore, as a punitive measure and partly for the sake of increased revenue, the Molasses Act was again renewed and broadened in what is known as the Sugar Act of 1764; and in 1765 and 1766 certain additional trade laws were passed, with the intention of reasserting the old rights of control over colonial commerce and of rendering it more profitable and advantageous to Great Britain. The chief object of this new regulation was, of course, to raise money wherewith to meet, in part at least, the heavy expenses likely to be incurred in administering and defending the new acquisitions in America.

These acts offered some relief to the merchants and planters living in America in the form of a reduction of duties and a granting of bounties, which show, as Beer has well said, "the desire of the British government to further the economic development of the colonies and its willingness to devote British funds to such purposes with the object of increasing the self-sufficiency of the empire." There can be no doubt that, as far as they affected trade, the laws were designed to encourage and not to restrict colonial industry; but they were energetically opposed by the merchants of New England, who at the first rumor in 1763 of the proposed renewal of the Molasses Act began systematically to attack it. Protests from the merchants of Massachusetts, Rhode Island, and Connecticut, and the remonstrance of the Rhode Island assembly, though unavailing, presented with admirable restraint and business-like brevity the grievances of the New Englanders and demonstrated with a wealth of facts and figures the inexpediency, as well as the injustice, of the act. The merchants of the Middle colonies were also affected, for, as Clement Biddle of Philadelphia said, in writing to Samuel Galloway, June 13, 1764, "The restrictions we are lay'd under by the parliament puts us at a stand how to employ our vessels to any advantage, as we have no prospect of markets at our own islands and cannot send elsewhere to have anything that will answer in return." As attempts were made to enforce the act and new acts were passed in 1765 and 1766, the complaints became more insistent, and powerful arguments were used to convince the British government that its policy, however well intentioned, was in reality unwise. The colonists called attention to the fact that the acts loaded their commerce with so many devices for preventing illegal trade and increasing the revenue, and granted such an extension of power to the customs officials, the vice-admiralty courts, and the officers of the navy in American waters as to cripple colonial trade and in the end destroy rather than relieve it. They urged with great force that there could be no advantage in measures which damaged the cause they were designed to benefit and cost more to carry out than the accruing revenues

Revolt of the Colonies

amounted to. The merchants in England also joined in the appeal and wrote letters to members of parliament and others recounting the injuries inflicted by England on their trade with America.

In these protests no one denied the right of parliament to pass these acts or made in any form the charge of constitutional illegality. The merchants in America based their objections solely on the ground of inexpediency, denouncing a governmental policy that affected Britons and Americans alike and did no good to either of them. As no question of parliamentary authority was raised, it is likely that in the long run their protests would have been successful; for Englishmen were generally willing to listen to trade grievances, and the colonial merchants, who as a rule were neither radical in temperament nor much addicted to politics, were open to any fair-minded settlement. But a peaceful issue was jeopardized at this juncture by an unexpected move on the part of parliament along new and ominous lines. I refer to the passage of the Stamp Act of 1765 and the Townshend Act of 1767.

Up to this time, parliament, though dealing with a wide range of colonial activities, had limited its interference chiefly to the regulation of commerce or to such matters as had to do with trade, manufacturing, and finance. In its first attempt to raise money wherewith to meet the demands of the new imperialism, it had endeavored to draw on an already existing source of income, that of colonial trade; but when it found this source to be inadequate and had to look elsewhere for funds, it made a new financial experiment in a colonial field hitherto untouched—that of direct taxation. The passage of a stamp act, therefore, was

Background of the Revolution

a deliberate attempt to secure the much needed revenue by the lightest known form of a direct tax, one that strictly speaking was not a tax at all, but rather a form of fee to be paid only for a definite service. Obtaining a revenue from this source had been tried by act of assembly in at least one of the colonies, New York, and had been recommended to the British authorities a number of times by British officials at home—such as Martin Bladen of the Board of Trade—and by British officials in America—such as Horatio Sharpe, governor of Maryland, and Henry McCulloh, formerly of North Carolina—who had become exasperated by the unwillingness of the colonial assemblies to aid the mother country during the French and Indian War. This obligation to buy stamped paper furnished by the home government or to imprint with a rubber stamp newspapers and pamphlets fell most heavily on the merchants, lawyers, and printers, and touched the Northern colonies more than it did those of the South or the West Indies. There can be no doubt but that at best the enforcement of this act would have caused a certain amount of hardship, requiring as it did a payment ranging from a halfpenny to ten pounds on a wide variety of transactions, intimately bound up with the daily life of the colonists; but the further provision of the law requiring that the payment be made in hard money—a commodity always scarce in the colonies and extremely so at this period, on account of the bad financial conditions prevailing nearly everywhere in America—aroused real alarm. The situation was further aggravated two years later, when parliament, by the passage of one of the Townshend Acts, placed an import duty on certain specified goods sent from Great

Revolt of the Colonies

Britain to America—glass, paper, painters' colors, white and red lead, and tea. This duty was a customs duty and so concerned trade, which parliament was accustomed to regulate; but it was similar to the stamp tax in the object for which it was imposed—the raising of a revenue—and in the medium of payment which it required—the sterling money of Great Britain, that is, gold, silver, or bills of exchange. However much Grenville and Townshend are to be condemned for their want of wisdom in carrying through at this juncture such unwelcome non-mercantilist legislation, there is no doubt but that they tried to burden the colonies as little as they could, one by imposing what he thought was an easy obligation and the other by avoiding anything suggestive of internal or direct taxation.

Two aspects of these laws are worthy of careful consideration. First, the financial aspect, to which little attention has hitherto been paid, though it had much to do with the hostility of the colonists to the measure. That which aroused apprehension in the colonies and created unrest was, in the beginning at least, the effect of the laws on the cost of living, their interference with the trade both at home and abroad, and their consequent menace to colonial prosperity. I venture to think that the mass of the colonial population bothered themselves but little with the intricate and subtle question of parliament's right to legislate for them, until that legislation touched intimately the daily condition of their lives. It is true that the question of "right" had become at this time a subject of more or less legal and metaphysical speculation, for one finds among the resolutions of the Stamp Act Congress certain philosophical declarations regarding the inherent rights of man.

Background of the Revolution

But these speculations, as well as the reasoned arguments and vigorous utterances of contemporary writers of a legal and meditative turn of mind—such as Otis, Hopkins, Dulany, and Dickinson—were of interest chiefly to intellectual circles. Newspapers and pamphlets had no widespread publicity, were limited as sources of news, and were inclined to controversy that often was long, verbose, and involved. The proceedings of the Stamp Act Congress itself, emblazoned as they are on the pages of history, passed almost unnoticed at the time, and there is nothing to show that the somewhat precise and finely spun reasoning of these intellectual leaders had any marked influence on the popular mind.

Thousands of the colonists never passed beyond the point of objecting to these acts because they seemed contrary to the fundamental laws of reason and justice, but agitators and propagandists, such as Samuel Adams, Christopher Gadsden, and others, who were searching for reasons wherewith to justify resistance, pushed the argument to its logical conclusion and often were able to use the results of their reasoning with telling effect upon a people already aggrieved and fearful of worse things to come. Only when the issues at stake found expression in popular phrases and slogans, such as "liberty versus oppression," "taxation without representation," and "the rights of man"—"stereotypes," these rallying cries have been called—did they become sufficiently a part of the experience and understanding of the average colonial inhabitant to stir in him the spirit of revolt. Conrad has expressed it well when he says, "Shouted with perseverance, with ardor, with conviction, [such words] by their sound alone have set whole nations in motion and upheaved the dry, hard ground on which rests our whole social fabric." Many of the points at issue in their logical and philosophical form were beyond the mental range of the colonist— even in New England, where the average intelligence was higher than elsewhere; but money and the means of subsistence were matters that concerned all and touched the lives of the poorest and most ignorant. The dislike which the colonists felt for the Stamp Act and the Townshend Act was due to their fear, as one address puts it, of being compelled "to give [Englishmen] our money, as oft and in what quantity they please to demand it," and as Count de Fersen said, in a moment of exasperation at the way the New Englanders fleeced the French soldiers, money was the "prime mover of all their actions." Once let the colonists believe that they were being unjustly treated by laws, whether of their own making or not, which threatened to drain them of what little circulating cash they had, and they were easily persuaded that these laws were not only ill advised but even unconstitutional. From this point it was but a short step to the conviction that parliament at any rate had no right to tax them at all, because in so doing it was encroaching on the lawmaking powers of their own assemblies. Hence the eventual cry of illegality and unconstitutionality.

In the second place, the Stamp Act and the Townshend Act were objectionable because of their effect on the balance of trade with Great Britain. A stamp tax on legal and other documents and an import duty on glass, paper, and other commodities would, if successfully collected, drain the colonies of their silver, and by just so much prevent the colonial merchants and planters from using this money to meet their trade balances. As early as January, 1764 Rhode Island had said, that should the Sugar Act be enforced "there is not so large a sum of silver and gold circulating in the colony, as the duty imposed by the aforesaid act upon foreign molasses would amount to in one year, which makes it absolutely impossible for the importers to pay it." That which was true in 1764 was none the less true in 1765, when the merchants of Philadelphia complained that "the several acts of parliament lately passed . . . have cut off from us all means of supplying ourselves with specie enough even to pay the duties imposed on us, much less to serve as a medium of our trade. If carried into execution they will further tend to prevent our making those remittances to Great Britain for payment of old debts or purchase of more goods, which the faith subsisting between the individuals trading with each other requires." A contemporary Connecticut writer expressed the same idea somewhat more quaintly. "If parliament," he said, "is convinced with me that the interests of Great Britain and her colonies are inseparable, they will not come into any plan to embarrass us in our trade, nor take from us the small remainder of a medium of trade by any scheme whatever, when they are already sure of having all we can possibly spare in the mercantile way; which with cheerfulness we have yielded them for their emolument, and which is highly probable will be the case for the future, if the genius of the people be duely attended to and properly encouraged." The British merchant was always worried about the collection of his debts in America and in a large majority of cases the colonial debtor was constantly struggling to square his accounts with Great Britain; while the pressure which the English or Scottish creditor brought to bear upon the merchant or planter in the colonies was passed on by the latter to the everyday man—the small householder, retail dealer, country store-keeper, farmer, and poor man generally—who bought on credit and was in a chronic state of arrears. Owing to the scarcity of hard money in the colonies and the tendency of paper to depreciate, the incurring of indebtedness was a prevailing habit with the colonists and suits for debt were matters of common occurrence. The situation became even more distressing after 1763, owing to the heavy obligations incurred in consequence of the war with France.

In England and Scotland also the period of the Stamp Act was a time when credit was much distressed by failures in the business world; when the merchants were complaining of advancing wages, increased cost of materials, and scarcity of goods; and when the landed classes were embarrassed by rising prices and a fall in the value of their lands. Whenever any question arose in parliament affecting mercantile interests in general, the British and Scottish merchants who traded with the colonies were always ready to exert their utmost strength in opposition to whatever, as they said in one instance, "would so much distress our friends in America," so it is not surprising that when the British government demanded sterling money for their stamp taxes and import dues, these merchants should have been ready to protest against acts which threatened the profits from colonial trade. They denounced the Stamp Act as an imperialist attack on colonial resources, a killing of the goose that was laying the golden eggs. In 1765 and

Background of the Revolution

1766 they appointed a committee "to make such application to the administration and parliament as should be thought necessary respecting the many restrictions and inconveniences attendant on the American trade"; applied to the secretaries of state and other persons in power for "their patronage" and received from them offers of assistance; sent circulars to all the manufacturers in the United Kingdom and a general letter to the merchants of Philadelphia and other colonial towns. Their efforts were rewarded not only by the repeal of the Stamp Act, but also by modifications of the Sugar Act and the trade act of 1765. To Alderman Trecothick, D. and J. Barclay, and Daniel Mildred, prominent merchants of London, was most of the credit due for the relief thus procured. The colonial merchants protested likewise, and in 1765 and again in 1768-1770 entered upon a series of non-consumption and non-importation measures that were designed to ease the financial situation and to bring the British government to terms. This, the first organized resistance in America to the financial policy of Great Britain and the real beginning of the movement for separation from the mother country, brought about what no amount of complaint on political or constitutional grounds could ever have effected, the repeal of a parliamentary statute. Great Britain could not afford to put in peril her greatest asset in America, which, as Lord North said afterwards, was "the basis of the wealth and power of the kingdom."

The repeal of the Stamp Act brought great satisfaction to the colonists, who in some quarters declared themselves to be still "faithful, dutiful, and loyal subjects" inspired by "willing subjection and unbounded love." Four years later the removal in part of the Townshend duties and Hillsborough's promise that the government would lay no further taxes on the colonies by act of parliament relieved the strain of a tense situation. Even the retention of the duty on tea did not excite colonial displeasure to any serious extent, for during the ensuing three years the duty in many cases was willingly paid and in others successfully evaded. But the course of events since 1764 had disclosed not only irreconcilable ways of thinking and feeling between the two countries but also ominous differences of opinion between the mercantile classes in general and the radicals in America, the latter of whom were already advancing grievances based on what they claimed were their constitutional rights.

The merchants on both sides of the water had been able to impress the British government with the fact that the passing of the Stamp Act and the Townshend Act was "contrary to the true principles of commerce," meaning thereby contrary to the best interests of mercantilism. But those who based their appeals on arguments of a constitutional or legal nature, as was done by the Stamp Act Congress and some of the colonial assemblies, were not so successful; for their addresses were either not admitted to parliament at all or else were rejected without consideration. The petition to the king from the New York assembly, presented to Lord Hillsborough by the agent, Robert Charles, was disapproved partly because it ought to have come through the governor and not directly from the assembly, but still more because it seemed "to draw into question the supreme authority of parliament to bind the colonies by laws in all cases whatsoever." In fact, the

more strongly the colonists stressed the so-called illegal
and unconstitutional encroachments of crown and parliament, the less responsive became the British merchants and
the less successful were they when they made their appeals
to parliament. It was nearly three years after the passage
of the Townshend Act before the merchants were able to
effect its repeal, and the reason for this delay is stated by
one of them when he wrote, in 1769, that had "a petition
come over from your merchants on the principle of expediency instead of from your assembly denying the right,
the law would ere now have been repealed." So strong was
the desire for a continuation of peaceful relations on the
part of thousands in Great Britain and America that the
moderates in both countries were able, for a time, to hold
the extremists in check; but the situation grew steadily
worse as the extremists in the colonies reiterated their constitutional claims. By 1775, as we shall see, the influence
of the merchants was entirely gone and their petitions
were all rejected.

The critical period of pre-Revolutionary history is from
1770 to 1774; and of the many conflicting influences at
work at this time—conservative, moderate, and radical—
no one can be ignored, if we would form a just estimate
of an intricate situation. In the past, writers on the pre-
Revolutionary period have overstressed the radical or patriotic side of the story and have neglected or dealt unfairly
with the opposing forces of conservatism and compromise,
apparently unable or unwilling to understand the British
side of the story.

The British habit of mind during this period and the
attitude of contemporary British writers toward the points

at issue can best be found in the utterances of men in the ministries, parliament, and such branches of government as the secretary of state's office for the southern department, the Privy Council, and the Board of Trade, which were officially in charge of colonial affairs. These men and hundreds of others in public life considered the colonies merely as plantations, contributing to British wealth and prosperity. They might differ as to the wisdom of imposing a stamp tax or the financial expediency of levying the Townshend duties, but they were all agreed in believing that there was only one status for a colony—the status of an outlying community, dependent on the mother country and subject to the authority of crown and parliament. Some of them still remained pure mercantilists, valuing the colonies only for the wealth they furnished and believing that the true end of all colonization was commerce. Others, already touched with the spirit of imperialism, looked upon the economic connection as merely a means to a higher political end. They were the ones who were largely responsible—a matter of the greatest importance in our discussion—for the Declaratory Act of 1766, a distinctly imperialistic measure, in that it asserted, as of right, the authority of king and parliament over the colonies and demanded of the colonists duty and obedience. Public opinion at large is never easy to discover, except as it is available in pamphlets, magazines, newspapers, and addresses of protest or loyalty. As it happened, unfortunately for the historian of to-day, only a small portion of the British population in the eighteenth century took any interest in public affairs and a still smaller number gave expression to their views in print. Nevertheless, it is fairly certain that very few Englishmen, and those only of strongly radical and speculative temperament, believed that colonies should be anything else than subordinate dependencies. An English correspondent of the year 1775, evidently a landowner and country gentleman, who may have represented the sentiment of many others of his class, gave utterance in print to an extreme view of the case. "The colonies," he writes, "may be considered as the great farms of the public and the colonists as tenants, whom we wish to treat kindly whilst they act as such; but when they usurp the inheritance and tell us they are and will be independent of us, it is time to look about us and keep them to the terms of their leases." Men holding such opinions might disagree among themselves and with those in authority as to how the colonies should be treated, but they could have no sympathy with the radical claims of America.

On the other hand there were doctrinaire writers who vitally disagreed with the government and vigorously denied parliament's right to levy an internal tax upon the colonies, while others—John Horne (later Horne-Tooke), for example—wished to grant the colonies control over all taxation, on the principle that they should enjoy the rights, liberties, and privileges of Englishmen. Still others —of whom the chief representatives were Thomas Pownall, John Cartwright, and Dr. Richard Price—were inclined to repudiate the doctrine of colonial dependency altogether, and to uphold the policy of freeing each colony from the authority of any other legislative body than its own. According to this view, which found supporters in America also—for Franklin seems to have had some such idea—the colonies could be held in subjection only by force; and it was far better for a permanent connection to be maintained by recognizing "the supreme legislature as existing in the majesty of the king, as the common head of all his parliaments, and exercising his authority with their consent, while no one of them encroaches on the rights of the rest." Josiah Tucker, Dean of Gloucester—a friend neither of the colonies nor of the British ministry, though a profound believer in the British constitution—was, like Thomas Pownall, convinced that some such imperial partnership would be advantageous to Great Britain and that colonies which could not accept their assigned place in the mercantilist scheme should be allowed to control their own legislative destinies. Occasionally there arose a prophet who saw the complete independence of America already written in the decrees of the fates.

But speculation of this kind regarding the equality of parliaments or the independence of the colonies, interesting as it is to the modern student of political theory, had no influence upon the course of events, for the advisers of government were not the philosophers but the lawyers. In 1766 it was said that all the eminent lawyers, with one exception—Lord Camden—were "clearly and strongly of the opinion that the British parliament has an undoubted right to tax America." To mercantilist and imperialist alike, the orthodox view of colonial dependency was a foundation stone of the British system and no amount of theorizing or speculation could alter the attitude of the government on this point. To suppose that the king would give up his prerogative or that parliament would resign its authority in the interest of some federal arrangement for

Background of the Revolution

the colonies, is to believe that the British governmental authorities of that day would act from philanthropic motives or under the spell of chimerical and utopian dreams.

American opinion inevitably was much less unanimous. First, among those who were opposed to extreme measures were the conservatives, British or colonial born, men who were actuated by sentiment rather than principle, were loyal to their oaths of allegiance to the king and sincerely believed in the existing constitutional order. They represented all grades of society, rich and poor alike; some held office under the crown and some contented themselves with private life. Secondly, there were the merchants and other members of the propertied class—Israel Pemberton and other wealthy Quakers of Philadelphia, for example—whose instincts were conservative, and whose preferences, little influenced by questions of political and constitutional theory, were for friendly coöperation with their fellow merchants of Great Britain in order to preserve a business connection that was profitable to all. Thirdly, there were those, neither bold enough nor reckless enough to court disaster, who opposed a declaration of independence, because they believed that an armed contest with Great Britain would end in defeat and the consequent ruin of the colonies. Among the members of all these groups were thousands who were patriotic at heart and devoted to America, whose moderate views were due not to moral cowardice or self-interest only, but to honest convictions and a natural instinct of self-preservation.

At the other extreme were the radicals, many of whom, in the South as well as the North in the days of the Stamp Act, had banded together as Sons of Liberty. At first these groups were composed of moderates and radicals alike, but later, as the movement advanced, only radicals remained, young and fiery souls with none too much respect for constituted authority and intensely antagonistic to all phases of British policy. They found their first supporters in the towns of eastern Connecticut and made up for the comparative fewness of their numbers by the warmth of their appeal and the activity of their popular associations. They did much to arouse the large body of colonial farmers who, living isolated and remote, were often indifferent and inert as far as political issues were concerned. Many of the more temperate among them—John Adams, Roger Sherman, William Samuel Johnson, and others—were high-minded, well educated, thoughtful men who, as someone has said, raised the issue from a mere dispute about money to the dignity of a cosmic event. Others—Christopher Gadsden, for example, the fighting cock of the South Carolina Commons House of Assembly—were radical by nature, and willing to sacrifice even their property interests for a cause in which they profoundly believed and which they upheld with a vociferousness that often bordered on hysteria. Still others were born political agitators, gifted with a genius for persuasion, propaganda, and organization, among whom was Samuel Adams, regarding whose merits the world will always be content to differ. Though straitened in pocket and unable to earn a living or support a family, he could with equal facility concoct plans amid the flip and the tobacco smoke of the Caucus Club in Tom Dawes's garret, sway the Boston town meeting with eloquent phrases, rouse the populace by the many varied devices of agitation congenial to his fertile and resourceful mind, and manipulate the political machine. Last of all were those whom the conservatives called the inferior sort, the populace, or the mob, to many of whom the colonies had never granted the right to vote, who bore few of the responsibilities of citizenship, paid a minimum of taxes, and were without property or civic obligations. They were the terrorists of the period, many of whom did their thinking in their muscles, and others, as Judge Keogh said of the chief justice of Ireland, used their jaws even more than they used their brains. Their influence lay in their physical ability to override law and order, destroy property, and intimidate their enemies, who in the absence of any adequate police organization in the colonies were unable to secure protection against violence.

Though no racial or religious lines of cleavage can be clearly discerned as marking a division of parties, nevertheless it is true that both racial and religious differences were at work intensifying party bitterness. Those who had fled to America to escape political oppression at home were bound to sympathize with any cause that had for its rallying cry "liberty and freedom." Scots-Irish, men of English stock, and Germans to a lesser extent—for in some quarters, as in North Carolina, the Germans played a neutral part during the Revolution—all alike were actuated by the strong radical feelings characteristic of the back country and the frontier, and in the main supported the cause of independence. The Highland Scots, on the other hand, were almost to a man on the side of the king and his authority. Generally speaking, Anglicans were loyalists and Dissenters radicals, but as not all Anglicans adhered to the British cause, so by no means did all Dissenters favor separation.

Revolt of the Colonies

From the time of the Stamp Act to the end of the year 1773—eight years—the moderates were in the saddle, able to control the movement and hold the radicals in check. They favored a policy of compromise and conciliation, hoping by passive resistance and by avoiding anything more drastic than non-consumption and non-importation measures to obtain a settlement of the dispute. Though willing to employ methods of legitimate coercion, they refused at first to raise the standard of constitutional revolt or resort to acts of revolution. "If we could be prudent," wrote Hutchinson, "I think I may say only silent, we might save the country and retain the rights we contend for, or which is the same thing, might rest assured that parliament would not exercise the right of taxing which they now claim and we may be assured will not give up. But if we go on denying the right and asserting our independence the nation will by force compell us to adopt it." Cushing voiced the same idea when he said, "Our natural increase in wealth and population will in the course of years settle this dispute in our favour, whereas if we persist in denying the right of parliament to legislate for us, they may think us extravagant in our demands and there will be great danger of bringing on a rupture fatal to both countries." Even Franklin had once championed expediency, when he bade the colonists "Manufacture as much as possible and say nothing." The British merchants in their advice to the colonists after the repeal of the Stamp Act in 1766 said that had the Americans but endeavored "to acquiesce with the law and dutifully represented the hardships as they arose," their relief "would have been more speedy and we should have avoided many difficulties as well as not a few unanswerable mortifying reproaches" on their account; and they expressed the hope that now the act was repealed, the colonists would comport themselves prudently and neither exult over parliament nor deem the result a colonial victory.

But the radicals scorned this doctrine of expediency and passive resistance as mercenary and pusillanimous. Said Sam Adams in answering Cushing, "When our liberty is gone, history and civilization alike will teach us that an increase in inhabitants will be but an increase of slaves." Repudiating the doctrine of passive obedience as "a tame submission to an unjust imposition," these men expressed their resentment against stamp distributors, non-subscribers, revolters, rescinders, lukewarm colonists, British sympathizers, and British officials in riots, mob actions, and the destruction of property, and even in the maltreatment of individuals. Such outbreaks show not only the ease with which liberty can degenerate into license, but also the absence, particularly in the town of Boston and the colonies of Connecticut and Rhode Island, of any efficient machinery for the enforcement of law and the maintenance of the public peace. Furthermore, the radicals, in their disgust with the excuse of expediency, asserted more loudly than before the unconstitutionality of the British position, charging the crown with injustice and parliament with exceeding its powers. Claims of this kind, found in the writings of individuals and the resolves of town meetings early in the sixties, became common after 1768, when "liberty versus slavery" was widely bruited as a radical slogan, threatening the permanent success of the policy of reconciliation. Probably few, if any, of the colonists at this juncture wanted, or even thought of, legal separation from Great Britain. Though political independence was undoubtedly discussed in private, it was neither suggested nor asked for in public address or official resolution. Even the radicals went no further than to demand a curtailment of the prerogatives of the crown and the powers of parliament, and a recognition of the colonies as self-governing communities, invested with the right to enjoy an independent political and economic life of their own. While the moderates expressed their opinions temperately and in the main with sobriety and restraint, the radicals presented their grievances through the medium of pamphlets, newspaper articles, petitions, speeches, and correspondence, in words that were sometimes sublime in their earnestness and sometimes scurrilous in their resort to defamation and slander. Written in the heat of passion, much of the radical literature of the period before 1774 is but the illogical and uncontrolled product of a movement that was fast approaching the stage of revolution.

We need not discuss here the merits or otherwise of the controversies that fill the columns of contemporary newspapers, or the acts of cruelty, physical and mental, that disclose the blind unreason of revolt; but we can say with confidence that outbreaks of this character were something that Englishmen could neither understand nor condone. Indignation among political leaders and in military and naval circles in England had already been aroused during the French and Indian War by the actions of the colonists, whose trading with the enemy, without shame or concealment, had done much to frustrate the policy of the British government and prolong the war. And now again ministries, members of parliament, public officials, and men of prominence generally were thoroughly angered by the constant iteration of this charge of "unconstitutionality" that appeared in the resolutions and petitions of colonial assemblies, for they construed it as a denial on the part of the colonists of the executive and legislative authority of the British government in all that concerned colonial affairs. Individuals in England denied the legality and even the justness of the colonial position; parliament made clear its dissent by passing the Declaratory Act and retaining the tax on tea; and Hillsborough, the secretary of state for the colonies, in his circulars to the governors, controverted in almost menacing language the colonial claims and pretensions. As the radicals in America persisted in their demands, as they advanced from arguments about trade to arguments about the civil rights of British subjects, and from these to arguments about inherent and self-evident rights according to nature, Englishmen in authority hardened their hearts, because in their minds recognition of the radical claim meant not only the wrecking of what they deemed their greatest asset in America, their profits from colonial trade, but more serious still the abrogation of their own constitutional system.

Despite the six years of excitement, agitation, and financial depression that followed the passage of the Sugar Act in 1764, and despite the intensity of feeling aroused in Great Britain and America by the Stamp Act riots, the nonimportation measures, the Boston "massacre," and other stirring events of this critical period, the years from 1770 to 1773 were a time of comparative calm. Business revived, commercial prosperity returned, the moderates had the situation well in hand, and the Sons of Liberty, who had greeted the collapse of the non-importation movement with vexation of spirit, were for the moment discredited and under a cloud. John Adams, John Hancock, Isaac Low, and other radical leaders and anti-parliament men withdrew temporarily from public life. Even the disturbance caused by the burning of the British revenue vessel, *Gaspee*, in Narragansett Bay near Providence in 1772, did not seriously derange the existing tranquillity, though it led to the passage by parliament of the first coercive act in that year. Tea came in, legitimately from England and illegitimately from Holland and St. Eustatius; and it is to be feared that even the radicals were not always scrupulous as to which variety they drank. With prosperity and good feeling in the air, less was heard of the tyrannous supremacy of parliament, the rights of man, and encroachments on liberty. Only the extremists were restless under the calm, unwilling to let sleeping dogs lie. In the autumn of 1772, Sam Adams, stirred to action by the general apathy, sought to revive and organize radical sentiment in Massachusetts and elsewhere, by raising the old cries of colonial rights and British oppression, freedom versus slavery, and the illegality of parliamentary rule. Through the agency of the Boston town meeting, he brought into existence the first committee of correspondence, a form of intercolonial communication that was destined to have far-reaching results. But even this incident passed for the moment without more than local interest.

British ministers had already made many blunders of policy, partly because of their inability to comprehend the significance of the colonial unrest and partly because they failed to understand the language used in America, which, vibrant as it was of "liberty" and "slavery," struck no answering chord of sympathy or discernment in the heart of the average Englishman. No one in Great Britain wished to oppress the colonies and it is to be doubted if anyone in office thought he was really doing so. Grenville had no other desire than to shape his measures so as to affront them as little as possible; and Charles Townshend, though a plunger in politics, believed that he had met the difficulty regarding internal and external taxation by imposing an import duty, and so keeping within the limits of that particular form of parliamentary legislation to which the colonies had never objected. None of the others concerned with the administration of the colonies were so fatuous as to seek their injury. But wrong impressions can be created by other means than deliberate acts of enmity. An attitude of condescension; an air of superiority; the superciliousness of the courtier toward the provincial; the treatment of a growing state as if it were an undeveloped agricultural plantation; a strict construction of British legal rights in America, which from the colonial point of view were obstructive and vexatious; an utter lack of understanding on the part of the British officials at home of the difficulties under which the colonists labored or of the true inwardness of the grievances from which they suffered—all of these things made for constant irritation and complaint. Jedediah Huntington of Connecticut, a brigadier-general in the Continental army, expressed a current colonial opinion of British officials generally when he said in 1778, speaking of the peace commissioners, "They never could bear to think us upon any equality with them, they know they can't subdue us, they can't love us, it is not in their nature. They will, I fancy, after a few frivolous attempts towards a reconciliation leave us to ourselves."

Even when concessions were made they were offered grudgingly and in a manner not likely to win the affection of the colonists. To Englishmen there were ample reasons why the trade laws should be enforced, why a revenue should be raised in America, why the mother country should be reimbursed for the assistance which the colonies asked for and expected, and why Canada and the western lands should be administered in the interest of the French habitants and the Indian tribes; but the colonies believed that these measures were deliberately contrived to injure them and benefit others. The proclamation of 1763 was construed as an attempt to prevent colonial expansion westward. The trade laws of 1765 and 1766 and the measures regarding the Newfoundland fisheries were resented because they hampered, unnecessarily the colonists thought, commercial freedom and opportunity. The Quebec Act was viewed as but a first step toward bringing Roman Catholicism upon the colonies and at best it seemed to imply that if parliament by statute could impose "popery" it could impose "episcopacy" also, a thing, as one correspondent said, "rather worse than a stamp duty." The establishment at Boston in 1768 of an American Board of Customs Commissioners, though defensible from the standpoint of British customs administration, added to the general irritation at a critical time by its very effectiveness. The quartering of troops in colonial houses and taverns "under pretence for our defence" was deemed rather "a rod and check over us," and aroused fears of

Background of the Revolution

coercion; while the enlargement of the vice-admiralty system in the same year and the erection of four new vice-admiralty courts at Halifax, Boston, Philadelphia, and Charleston, with both original and appellate jurisdiction, seemed to portend a permanent tightening of the imperial bonds. No wonder that many of the colonists longed for the good old easy days before 1764 and looked with apprehension to the future. Furthermore, the British officials of this period in America, in civil administration, the vice-admiralty courts, and the customs service, with whom the colonists came into close and frequent contact, were rarely tactful men capable of relieving the local discontent by a considerate handling of difficult and awkward situations.

However, in the summer of 1773, the outlook for peace was encouraging. As far as one could see the most dangerous crisis had passed; the moderates had the situation well in hand and the radicals were losing rather than gaining ground. It was a time for the British ministry to tread warily in order not to disturb a delicately balanced state of affairs. But this seemed to be the very thing that the ministers, short-sighted, ponderous, and self-centered, were unable to do. At this critical juncture, probably with the best of intentions and with no realization of the ultimate consequences, Lord North and his cabinet committed an irretrievable blunder.

The facts are these. In May of 1773 parliament had passed an act designed to relieve the East India Company, the greatest tea importing concern of the time, of what seemed to be a serious financial embarrassment. The company having accumulated a large surplus stock was in danger of bankruptcy, and that it might enlarge its market and dispose of its accumulation, parliament granted to it what was equivalent to a monopoly of the tea trade to America. Under the terms of the act, the company was permitted to ship its tea directly to the colonies in its own vessels, thus cutting out the independent British or colonial importer; and to sell it in the colonies through selected consignees, who were to act as branch agencies of the company, thus cutting out the independent colonial merchant, who in the past had been accustomed to handle this commodity himself. Under the favorable terms of this act, these branch agencies would be able to sell more cheaply than the regular merchants, more cheaply even than the dealers who had been wont to traffic in the smuggled article. The method used was the now familiar one of eliminating the middleman and his profits by allowing the producer or exporter to sell directly to the consumer. How far the scheme was justified by the condition in which the company found itself it is difficult to say. We are told that in a discussion which took place in the House of Commons in 1774, Governor Johnstone reminded Lord North of an earlier private conversation, in which he (Johnstone) had said that the sending of the tea to America could be of no service to the company and was certain to be resented by the colonists. Johnstone was partly right in his forecast, for the scheme aroused the immediate and widespread opposition of those who saw only that a monopoly privilege had been gratuitously conferred upon an outside and, as they believed, a grasping corporation. The fact that they could purchase the tea at half its usual price did not in the least diminish their indignation.

For the first time an issue had arisen which affected

moderates and radicals alike. The merchants in the Northern colonies saw ruin staring them in the face, for not only were they threatened with the loss of their profits on tea, but were confronted also with the probability that the same company or other companies would be granted monopolies in such commodities as silks, drugs, and spices, all of which were essential articles in colonial life. They feared, as one of them wrote, that should this be the outcome, "America would be prostrate before a monster that may be able to destroy every branch of our commerce, drain us of all our property, and wantonly leave us to perish by thousands." The conservative New England merchants and the radical Sons of Liberty now found themselves linked together in a common cause. The monopoly of the East India Company threatened the business of the one, as the three pence a pound duty, which was still retained, threatened as "tribute" the "liberty" of the other. Both were facing what they believed to be a common danger—bondage to a power outside themselves.

This alliance of the moderate and radical in a common grievance was in every way unfortunate for the cause of reconciliation. If the more conservative merchants of New England still hoped to procure a withdrawal of the monopoly by an appeal to the old doctrine of expediency, they had reckoned without an adequate appreciation of the strength of the radical elements. So intense was their resentment because of the monopoly granted the East India Company that they departed for the moment from the policy of previous years and joined forces with the uncompromising popular party. But unable to control the situation, as they had done in 1766 and 1770, they soon found themselves carried beyond their depth on the crest of a radical wave that was far too powerful for them. Sam Adams and other revolutionary leaders of the town meetings of Boston and its neighborhood were determined to force a crisis. The radicals scored their first victory and lessened the chances for reconciliation on December 16, 1773, when they destroyed £10,000 worth of the East India Company's property in Boston harbor. This famous episode, known as the Boston Tea Party, was a spectacular performance, which in its wanton violation of private property found its equal elsewhere only in the burning of the *Peggy Stewart* in Annapolis harbor, an even less commendable affair, because thereby not only the company's tea was destroyed but the consignee's ship as well. The attitude of the merchants of the south toward the Boston event is shown in a letter from William Wiatt of Fredericksburg, Virginia, to his brother in Liverpool. "Don't imagine me prejudiced," he wrote, "when I say they [the people of Boston] deserve worse treatment from the hands of the English; their manner of proceeding was so unlike men of spirit and resolution. In the disguise of Indians they went and destroyed the property of a Company, who had the liberty of sending their commodities to any of his Majesties British Colonies in America. If they found it a premeditated design in Government to tax the people, it was their business to have stored the tea, let it lie in the public warehouse and rot; the duty must have been paid by the persons to whom it was consigned, at such a period, and it was in their power either to purchase or let it remain at the risk of the consignees; but they are a cunning designing set; they were afraid it would hurt their smuggling trade with Statia [St. Eustatius]." The Charleston collectors succeeded in storing the first tea that arrived in vaults without opposition, though as the excitement increased a few chests of a later consignment were thrown into the Cooper River. The Quakers in Philadelphia sent back their tea ship without unloading as the Boston people would probably have done, had not Governor Hutchinson, who was himself interested in the consignment, unwittingly played into the hands of Adams and Molineux, both uncompromising radicals and professional agitators, by forbidding the ship to leave the harbor. It is an interesting fact that the merchants of Portsmouth, "detesting every idea of violating property," protected the tea even when refusing to receive it; and that John Dickinson, author of the *Farmer's Letters,* disapproved of the Boston outbreak and in so doing brought down upon himself the wrath of Adams and other radical Bostonians who were largely responsible for the outrage and who, more than any one else, brought radical sentiment to fever heat in 1773. For a time the moderates in Great Britain, shocked and disillusioned by the wanton destruction, believed that the first Continental Congress would recompense the East India Company for the tea destroyed; but even had America been in a mood for so honorable a course, Sam Adams would have opposed it with his dying breath.

The crisis which had been averted for ten years was now come without hope of evasion. The irreconcilable element in the colonies threw down the gauntlet to the mother country and with equal grimness of temper Great Britain took up the gage. The quarrel entered the third and final stage of its history. It was no longer concerned with the old mercantile question of trade, or even with the imperial question of revenue; it had reached that most fundamental of all issues, the status of the colonies and their political and legal relations with the mother country. As early as 1766, Lord Lyttelton, when opposing the repeal of the Stamp Act, had said with prescience, "This is no question of expediency; it is a question of sovereignty until the Americans submit to the legislature." Were the colonies to remain perpetually subject to the will of the mother state, or might there be discovered some higher form of relationship, in which mother country and daughter land could find mutual profit and contentment, without weakening the ties that bound them? Events for a decade had shown that the American colonies were striving, half unconsciously, half purposely, to assert their status as self-governing communities, but these same events had also shown that the British government was unable to offer any new solution of the problem that confronted them.

There were those in England, just as there were those in America, who in their effort to interpret the facts as they saw them spoke of the relationship between Great Britain and the colonies in terms of a federation or partnership of states, pursuing separate courses under a common sovereign and linked commercially by mutually advantageous agreements. But the time had not come for those in authority or even for Englishmen generally to contemplate or conceive an arrangement based on any other principle than one of colonial dependence and submission. Contemporary statesmen, with the responsibilities of government on their shoulders, could not have entertained for a moment a colonial policy which took from Great Britain all legislative authority over her colonies and left them free to elect their own magistrates, enact their own laws without supervision, and adopt such regulations regarding trade and manufacturers as they might think proper. Such a policy, as Adam Smith said, never had been and, according to the official ideas of the time, never could be put into practice by any nation in the world. The very concessions that might have prevented the American Revolution would, in the eyes of British statesmen, have impaired the prosperity of the empire by rendering the colonies valueless to Great Britain. Had these men, whom we condemn so easily, at any time seriously considered an independent status for the colonies, they would have found themselves on the horns of a troublesome dilemma—should they retain the colonies, they would have to enter upon such a compromise as would destroy the value of the colonies as a source of income, and in so doing would violate one of the most fundamental tenets of the mercantilist faith. On the other hand, should they refuse to compromise, a rupture would certainly follow which, as Adam Smith said again, would be of such a sort as to strike "the people of Great Britain with more terror than they ever felt for a Spanish armada or a French invasion."

This conflict of antagonistic interests between the mother country and the colonists had its inevitable result. The quarrel became, in all its naked hideousness, an open rupture, characterized by defiance on one side and coercion on the other. The accumulated grievances of ten years, fanned into flame by the almost fanatical persistence of the Boston radicals, had culminated in a lawless assault on the property of a private company and an act of insult to the majesty of the British crown and parliament. Just as the monopoly grant to the East India Company had strengthened the hand of the extremists in America, so the destruction of the tea in Boston harbor gave the control of affairs in England to those whose resentment had been rising steadily since the French and Indian War and whose growing influence at this juncture destroyed all hope of compromise among the friends of America, both in and out of parliament. The reply to the Boston Tea Party was the act of March 31, 1774, which closed the port of Boston, and the further acts of May 20, which reduced Massachusetts to the status of a crown colony and ordered that all persons indicted for murder or other capital crimes be sent to England or some other colony for trial.

These acts were received with consternation in America, as "subversive of the liberties of this wide extended continent"; and a memorial to the general assembly of Connecticut expressed extreme apprehension lest the colonies should be "under the disagreeable necessity of defending our sacred and inviolable rights, sword in hand, for we would not entertain a thought that any American would or possibly could be dragooned into slavery." Immediately the demand arose for concerted action, and the first Continental Congress, consisting of fifty-six delegates, met at Philadelphia, September 5, 1774. In the election of members the moderates made their last conspicuous effort to recover their control of the situation. Thomas Ringold, writing to Samuel Galloway, June 18, said, "I return from congress of committees [at Annapolis for the election of delegates and other purposes]. I think as many moderate people as possible should be there to unite their influence to prevent resolves for non-exportation as well as non-importation, the first of which would certainly only serve to render our province contemptible even in the opinion of our neighbors and it would be setting ourselves up a mark for ministerial vengeance." But this effort in Maryland and elsewhere met with slight success. A considerable number of those chosen were favorable to the radical cause, though no one could tell beforehand what they were likely to do because their instructions were largely confined to matters of redress and made no provision for constructive organization or measures of resistance. But the extremists, headed by Sam Adams, soon took the lead, and in what they accomplished exemplified the truth of Lord Bacon's aphorism on factions, that "It is often seen that a few that are stiff do tire out a greater number that are more moderate." They demonstrated the ability of a small, determined, and uncompromising minority, well organized and astutely led, to win a victory over a large and less wieldy majority of varying minds and diverse interests, whose views at this time probably represented the views of the greater part of the colonial population. Though the congress drafted petitions and presented grievances, its most significant act was the adoption of the Continental Association—a non-intercourse measure on a larger scale, similar to that which Adams had been advocating ever since the Port Act went into effect. This measure it imposed on the colonies not as a matter of local option through legitimate agencies, but as something to be obeyed by all. Local extra-legal radical organizations—committees of public safety and the like—were already in existence, prepared to put this order into force and compel acquiescence by means of intimidation and the boycott. Thus the work of the congress was a defeat for the moderates and the mercantile interests, in that its most important measure was not one of reconciliation but of challenge, differing from earlier nonimportation agreements in that it compelled those who were lukewarm or out-and-out British supporters to make a positive declaration of their position. Radicalism was rapidly acquiring a complete control of the situation.

Four months later came the first clash of arms at Lexington and Concord. Economic pressure gave way to armed revolt, and the radical boycott was replaced by aggressive terrorism, accompanied by fines, imprisonments, and threats of bodily injury. The new issue completely broke up the old party groups in the colonies and rendered a new alignment inevitable. The moderates disappeared, for there existed no longer a middle ground between those who upheld the British policy of coercion and those who believed, unreservedly, that the colonies were justified in their resistance. Those who refused to follow the radical lead or to accept without qualification and without delay the cause of revolution were branded as enemies to their country and labeled without discrimination loyalists and tories. Though final decisions were not always reached at once, and though many incidental influences combined to operate in individual cases—such as self-interest, family connections, personal likes and dislikes, and fear of the "swift wrath" of the radicals—yet before the Declaration of Independence had made the decision irrevocable, the moderate party, as far as we can call it a party, had begun to disintegrate. Those holding office under the crown; conservatives who hated revolution and believed in the enforcement of law and order; colonial merchants who feared that radicalism meant anarchy and the end of peace and prosperity; and all who preferred to remain loyal to the king and the constitution now swung into line on the British side and became the Loyalists of the Revolution.

On the other hand, many of the moderates, influenced by patriotic motives, governed by a spirit of self-seeking, stricken with fear for their lives or property, or else honestly convinced that Great Britain was the enemy of human rights and liberty, threw in their lot with the radical cause of independence. Thus vanished, as a mediating factor in the struggle, the merchant class, which for ten years had sought by every means in its power to prevent a rupture with the mother country. This result was not attained without bitterness and suffering. With all allowance for partisan exaggeration, General Gage, writing to Lord Dartmouth, was not far from the truth when he said: "There is no kind of tyranny and cruelty that these pretenders to freedom and liberty don't exercise over those in their power, who oppose their schemes tho' only by words. No man dares speak his sentiments and many are forced into the rebel troops, having no alternative but to take arms or go to gaol, and from what we hear from other places this despotic conduct is general." Nor were the Loyalists the only ones who suffered, for many an American patriot who loaned his government money to aid the cause of independence never received back either principal or interest, and was compelled to live out his later years in poverty and distress.

The issue on both sides was sharply drawn. In America pleas for a compromise based on mutual commercial advantages were cried down as mercenary, unpatriotic, and inimical to the cause of liberty. Suggestions in the newspapers that the king be recognized as the "complete head of all his parliaments," though finding supporters in both countries because representing actual conditions, were impossible of acceptance in America, where the movement had gone beyond the stage of compromise, and passed unheeded in Great Britain, where the government was bent on coercion. Plans for an imperial union, such as that outlined by Galloway and the moderates in the first Continental Congress, were rejected and the entry in Galloway's case was expunged from the minutes. The radicals wanted no amicable settlement of the difficulty; they wanted no executive of any kind, much less one who would exercise his prerogative from a vantage point three thousand miles away. "Liberty" to them had come to mean complete control of their own governments, free from the intervention of any external body whatever; while "despotism" they defined as any limitation upon the conduct of their own affairs imposed by established authority, under a pretext of right based on prerogative, statute, or charter.

The views of the British authorities were no less definite. They construed "liberty" as rebellion, and the claims of the colonists as a defiance of the law and the constitution. When the merchants of England and Scotland, frightened by the adoption of the Continental Association and confronted with the loss of their trade and the money due them in America, sought to obtain the repeal of the acts of 1774 and to prevent the passage of further retaliatory measures, they found their influence gone and their petitions rejected. Many were alienated from the American

cause by the excesses of the radicals there; some were lukewarm in their attitude; others found that the complaints
of business depression, already become serious in 1775, had
lost their force and were barren of results. The North ministry, in no mood for concessions, determined to meet blow
with blow. Convinced that the question was no longer one
of trade or revenue but of the authority of the British constitution itself—as Solicitor-General Wedderburn
frankly acknowledged—it refused even to consider the
"Petition" from the first Continental Congress, which
George III had referred to parliament. "If the Americans," said Lord North, "refuse to trade with Great Britain they shall trade nowhere else"; and in 1775 he carried
through parliament three retaliatory measures, the last
of which prohibited the thirteen rebellious colonies from
trade and intercourse with any part of the world and rendered their ships liable to seizure as if they had been the
ships of an enemy. On both sides of the water, the extremists were in command, grim and unyielding. The
breach that began in 1773 steadily widened, as one event
after another drove the contesting forces along divergent
lines of coercion and defiance. Massachusetts only was
affected by the acts of 1774; the whole of New England
was disciplined by the Restraining Act of 1775; but the
entire group of the rebellious colonies was placed under
a commercial ban by the Prohibitory Act of the same year.
In their turn the radicals in America were quick to respond,
and the Continental Association, the battles of Lexington
and Concord, and the Declaration of Independence were
but progressive acts of defiance. The first was commercial,
the second military, and the third political, but all were

Revolt of the Colonies

steps toward the complete severing of constitutional and legal relations with the mother country. The two countries were facing revolution, with all its bitterness and suffering, and with its disorganization, destruction, and terror. As Professor Harlow has well said in his *Life of Samuel Adams,* "The results of a revolution may be of the utmost value, once the necessary adjustments can be made, but the process of achieving them is sure to work like slow torture upon a considerable portion of the population."

But neither the controlling groups in Great Britain nor those in America took into consideration any such matters as these nor would they accept any measures looking to compromise or conciliation. The *impasse* was complete, and the only solution that remained was war. This they adopted, and the War of the American Revolution which followed ended in the independence of the colonies and the inauguration of a great experiment in self-government, commensurate in its significance for the human race with the equally great experiment in colonization which England had begun in the seventeenth century.

IV.
General Reflections

General Reflections

EFORE passing to a consideration of the American Revolution and its causes, it is necessary to comment briefly upon the influences, subjective and otherwise, which in the past have governed much writing upon these topics and which continue to characterize the attitude of many people toward them at the present time. The scholar's approach to the study of these critical years of our history is beset with many a pitfall and impeded by many a tangled obstruction in the form of myths and legends which have grown up about the principal events and characters. He who is accustomed to the open door of opportunity in nearly all other fields of historical investigation is always disconcerted by the half-truths that often pass current for history in this country, and by the opposition aroused and the criticism excited, when in all honesty he tries to discover the truth for himself. Perhaps he is discouraged chiefly by the lack of interest which prevails very widely among the American people in that reinterpretation of our history which is very greatly needed and which is bound to take place as historical knowledge increases, historical standards improve, and a better understanding is reached of the problems involved. In some instances this lack of interest is due to sheer apathy, in others to a complacent satisfaction with our history as it is now written, and in still others to a deliberate attempt to block revision of judgments by those whose interest it is that the older version be preserved.

Among the chief obstructions that one meets in the attempt to popularize accurate interpretations of our pre-Revolutionary and Revolutionary periods is propaganda, harmless in a way because only temporary and certain to lose its force with the disappearance of the cause that provoked it, but constantly reappearing in new guises. As new issues arise, propagandists find in our revolutionary movement precedents and parallels available for their arguments, while others use it to keep alive the ancient grudge against Great Britain. Quite long enough has misunderstanding and ill will been perpetuated in this country by the anti-British textbooks in use in our schools and by the anti-British politicians, who pretend to see in any attempt at fairness an evidence of a pro-British influence. The flame has been fanned by the teachings of Bancroft and his followers; by the memories of the Civil War, when Northerners resented the persistent, almost malignant, hostility of the British upper classes, and Southerners were angered by Britain's turning her back upon them when they began to lose; and, in more recent years, by an antagonism due to Great Britain's relations with Ireland and certain issues of the Great War. Propaganda of this sort does not yield readily to treatment, for as Mr. Wells says and truly, "Men who would scorn to tell a lie in everyday life will become unscrupulous cheats and liars when they have given themselves up to propagandist work." This habit of twisting, warping, and perverting history is perhaps more disastrous when indulged in to defend a cause, than when it is consciously exercised in

General Reflections

order to make a plea or sustain a point. Almost every religious body, conservative or liberal party, or radical group misuses history in its appeal to precedent; and among the advocates of many popular movements are always some who cleverly manipulate the history of the past in their desire to give an air of ancientry to their ideas and to find a precedent furnishing a warrant for action.

The second obstacle is the fondness of our American people for the worship of their ancestors and the cult of their heroes and their tendency to envelop men and events connected with our colonial past in an atmosphere of piety, patriotism, and perfection. In our desire to exalt local personages and to raise those of older days above the level of ordinary mortals, we are apt to forget that the men and women of our Revolution were little better or little worse than those who walk the earth to-day, and that their conduct must be judged by the conditions of their own times and not by the circumstances and ideas of a century and a half later. All good Americans are expected to believe that the achievement of independence and the creation of the Federal Constitution were, to use Professor Dunning's phrase, "the culmination of God's wonder-working in the life of mankind," and that both these events must in consequence have been the work of incredibly exemplary beings, possessed of more than ordinary human traits and abilities. People thus convinced of the sacrosanct character of any part of their past history are sure to resent the intrusion of the truth seeker and to make at least a show of indignation whenever the historian questions judgments already accepted as divine truths. Fortunately the American public is more receptive to-day to the truth of its own history than it was twenty-five years ago and will come in time and in increasing numbers to realize that the facts of its history, whether colonial, revolutionary, or national, are more inspiring and enlightening than are the exaggerations and fictions built up and defended by propagandist and hero-worshiper.

The third obstacle lies in the partisanship always exhibited by those who interpret history along patriotic lines. In the past, writers have endeavored to justify rather than to explain our Revolution, and in so doing have demonstrated the truth of the historical axiom that those who are seeking mere justification will never deal accurately with any subject. Such writers study but part of the evidence and fail to see that there are two sides to the story; or else prefer the kind of history which glorifies their country's past, and deem it less than one hundred per cent Americanism to dim in any way their country's achievements. The number of those who write this American brand of history or who demand that it shall be written for their children, is greater than one would readily suppose, and some striking instances of such human obliquity could be given. It is impossible to be fair and impartial if we study, as is usually done, only the American or revolutionary side of the story; or if we persist in extolling without discrimination all who supported the revolution, often glorifying as "patriots" lawless men who were nothing more than agitators and demagogues. The American sense of fair play and a square deal is not going to deny forever a hearing to the conservative side and to condemn almost unheard the cause that was lost. The established order, then as to-day, has a right to defend itself; and, in harmony with the prevailing attitude among historians, which moves them to look for truth on both sides of a controversy, it is the duty of the scholar in history to present its claims. There is ample evidence to show that an increasing number of those to-day who are interested in our early history are willing to view the case impartially, for though the summing up of the judge always lacks the excitement and picturesqueness of the plea of the advocate, it is equally true that a picture of embodied perfection is distasteful to the majority of mankind.

The fourth and most serious obstacle is the disinclination of the average American reader to take any interest in phases of our history that will have to be thoroughly and comprehensively examined before the causes of our Revolution can be understood. As a rule the hero-worshiper is repelled by the laborious methods of scientific investigation, and it has been well said that "hero-worship is always impatient of effort expended on the study of institutional, economic, or psychological phenomena, and its votaries are unfitted by temperament to measure the value of any other influences than those that are expressed in terms of biography." To interpret and reconstruct the life of the past one must have a lively imagination and the ability to sift and check up critically all evidence, of whatsoever kind it may be. To the average reader scientific history makes no appeal. He distrusts the critical scholar much as the politician distrusts the expert, and objects to high thinking and mental overstrain. He seeks in history mental relaxation rather than mental effort and gathers his impressions as he runs. His judgments are frequently inaccurate because based on secondary and often trivial evidence. General readers rarely go to the root of a matter or seek to discover the deeper purposes or principles involved, and are usually without that inquisitive scepticism which drives the scholar on and on in the search for truth. There are times when one fears that the public at large does not care for any other version of our history than that which already exists and is content to continue reading the same old story, provided it be salted and savored to taste. There are times, too, when one is inclined to agree with what Anatole France says in his preface to *L'Ile des Pingouins*:

"A quoi bon, mon pauvre monsieur vous donner tant de peine, et pourquoi composer une histoire, quand vous n'avez qu'à copier les plus connues, comme c'est l'usage? Si vous avez une vue nouvelle, une idée originale, si vous présentez les hommes et les choses sous un aspect inattendu, vous surprendrez le lecteur. Et le lecteur n'aime pas à être surpris. Il ne cherche jamais dans une histoire que les sottises qu'il sait déjà. Si vous essayez de l'instruire, vous ne ferez que l'humilier et le fâcher. Ne tentez pas de l'éclairer, il criera que vous insultez à ses croyances. Les historiens se copient les uns les autres. Ils s'épargnent ainsi de la fatigue et évitent de paraître outrecuidants. Imitez-les et ne soyez pas original. Un historien original est l'objet de la défiance, du mepris et du dégoût universels."

Conditions are, perhaps, not quite so bad as this in America, yet even here the quotation has its application. There are those who see in our history nothing but dramatic episodes and soul-stirring actions; who view our colonial era as a tangled mass of genealogical tree roots; who search in our past, as one would in a junk pile, for historical trivialities about which to dispute; or who have no higher concern than to demonstrate the superiority of a particular indi-

General Reflections

vidual, event, or colony over all the others. Such people, whether writers or readers, are certain to generalize from insufficient data and to be satisfied with explanations and conclusions which in their ignorant disregard of vital forces at work in the fields of industry, commerce, and finance, seem to the scholar glaringly inaccurate.

The popular tendency to be easily satisfied with history as it is written, as long as it tells an interesting story or deals with biography and dramatic achievements, is surpassed only by the similar popular tendency to interpret the past in the light of the present and to pay no attention to the changes that have taken place in the uses of words and the intrinsic character of ideas. While it is a commonplace to say that words have passed through a great variety of meanings in the history of their usage and that to our forefathers the terms "liberty," "democracy," "independence," and "representation," and the like connoted something quite different from what they mean in the language of to-day, it is not so readily grasped that social, political, and economic opinions also have passed through many stages of development in reaching their present state. Unless one follows the evolution of ideas and institutions in detail, one is almost certain to read into the words and phrases of our ancestors meanings that did not exist, thereby ascribing to men of a much earlier period not a little modern achievement. The average man who reads colonial history is in far too much of a hurry to consolidate or crystallize our national institutions and political ideas, and as a rule is much too modern to know the thoughts that our forebears were thinking—the common thoughts about common things.

Writers in the past have neglected all too much those

periods of silent revolution that are so often met with in the world's history, during which men's views, habits, and conditions of life have undergone almost imperceptible alterations, and the men themselves, doing their usual day's work, have been wholly unaware that they were playing an important rôle in a great social and economic transformation. Over and over again has the world waxed and waned while functioning in its customary everyday manner, and to discover what is happening during these periods of peaceful evolution is one of the most difficult of the many difficult tasks confronting the historian. He must study not only the documents that lie open to the inspection of all, but also the thousands of lesser records that concern the "forgotten man" and his ordinary existence. There are many periods of history when important structural modifications of the social order are brought about not by the professional reformer or the heroic leader of men, but by the people, high and low, who are meeting the need of their daily lives and are effecting constant readjustments, such as are necessary to keep the social body healthy and solvent.

Among these periods of silent and peaceful revolution must be counted the century and more leading up to our pre-Revolutionary movement. There are few eras in all history in which heroes and episodes are of so little relative importance as that from 1660 to 1765; nor can it be interpreted properly if approached from the standpoint of biography only. Its significance for British colonization lies not in the men it produced, but in the experiments it tested, the institutions it developed, and the ideas to which it gave rise. The very complexity of this period of our history

General Reflections

probably explains why it has been so inadequately treated in our textbooks and is so uninteresting to the average child at school; why it has been so little understood by the grown-ups; and why there has been such a strong tendency to make overmuch of the individuals concerned in particular movements, to take them out of their settings, and to clothe them with attributes that serve our liking and our pride. Nothing is easier than to endow our ancestors with the minds and manners that we would like them to have had and that some people think they ought to have had. Excessive devotion to biography leads almost inevitably to panegyric or abuse, and to the ascription of motives that are frequently purely imaginary. I have read school children's essays in which George III is pictured as a monster of wickedness, responsible for the Revolution and the loss to Great Britain of her colonies; and I have wondered whether even a child might not be taught that single individuals, no matter how important, do not create or stop revolutions at will, however much they may influence them, and that to charge a single man or even a group of men with responsibility for a great uprising like the American Revolution is to accept a trivial explanation for what in reality is a mighty cosmic event.

The American Revolution was a world movement far more important than the Revolution of 1689 in England and only equaled as a factor in the world's progress by the French Revolution of 1789. Its causes must be sought for deep down in the hearts and minds of a people, and not of one people only, but of two, for there are always two sides to a revolution. In studying the revolt of the American colonies we are dealing with two different types or states

of political and social development, which were the results
of environment and historical evolution and exhibit differences not merely of external conditions but of frames
of mind and ways of living as well. In our Revolution,
as in all revolutions, two great and powerful influences
came into conflict, the conservative and the radical, each
with its habits, impulses, and principles, and there can be
no real comprehension of causes and results unless each is
studied with equal thoroughness and care. No matter with
which side we happen to be in sympathy, we are in all
justice bound to try, at least, to understand the other. I
am never quite sure that those who are loudest in their
approval of the Declaration of Independence would be
among the revolutionists were they to face a similar issue
to-day, or that those who talk most insistently about patriotism would have been among those whom they love to
call the "patriots of '76." Are we consistent in glorifying
revolution in the past and abhorring it in the present or in
ennobling many of those who committed acts that to-day
we would execrate as offenses against law and order?
"Dead radicals," says a recent writer, "are eulogized because the issues for which they fought are as dead as the
men who advocated them. Belief in them has become
traditional and therefore eminently respectable." To this
truism may be added the further one, that a revolutionist
who is unsuccessful is likely to be condemned as a criminal,
whereas he who succeeds is sure to be dubbed a patriot, a
statesman, a hero, or a saint. It is always too much for human nature to glorify the losing side.

In the preceding essays we have already discussed the
historical antecedents of our Revolution. We have seen

how for a hundred years before that event the colonies and the mother country were moving in exactly opposite directions, each in obedience to historical tendencies that could not be resisted, the former toward intensive self-government, the latter toward empire. We have seen how the colonies, self-absorbed and preoccupied with their domestic problems, were gradually and almost insensibly outgrowing their status as dependencies and becoming self-conscious independent communities. Just because they were the most important and most advanced of all Great Britain's overseas territories, they were fully competent to have a separate life of their own, even though they remained bound politically and legally to the mother country. In these hundred years they had passed through a silent revolution with so little outward evidence of the fact as to make it sometimes difficult for us to follow it in all its bearings. Their inhabitants knew very little of the world outside themselves or of the interests of the mother country across the sea, and among them were very few who understood at all the difficulties of Great Britain's position after 1763 or realized any better than did the Britons themselves the new status of the British empire. So little did they comprehend it that in 1778, during a momentary lull in what has been called the second hundred years' war with France, they entered into an alliance with the French against their own mother country, and later won their independence through the aid of England's greatest colonial and commercial rival. It is not always easy to feel satisfied with the thought that we won our independence through the aid of a power that was using us for its own ends; and despite the fact that events of the Great War have thrown a glamour of romance about our relations with France in colonial times, it is difficult not to become a little cynical regarding that early alliance. Individuals like Lafayette undoubtedly had genuine sympathy for the American colonists and the issues they were facing; but the French government had no such interest in American independence. What France saw was an excellent opportunity to resume the war with Great Britain and, by aiding the colonies to obtain their freedom, to cripple her traditional enemy who had beaten her in the Seven Years' War.

On the other hand, Great Britain, with no clear-cut comprehension of where she was going, was moving toward territorial expansion and the establishment of an imperial policy and system. After 1763 the ministers were endeavoring, often with bewilderment and unconcealed dismay, to meet heavy demands for the defense and administration of large additions of territory, without adequate resources except through increased taxation. The British ruling classes, comprising less than one in fifty of the people of England—or if we take those actually in office, less than one in ten thousand—were concerned chiefly with external problems, and were paying very little attention to the domestic needs of the British people. Thus in England the period of our Revolution is one barren of internal reforms either in government or social life. Prominent Englishmen of the day were not burdening their minds with perplexing domestic questions any more than they could help, for in that selfish and scheming age the conscience of the English aristocracy and well-to-do gentry had not been awakened to the inequalities, the miseries, and the low standards of living that existed among the masses of England.

General Reflections

Here were divergent and antagonistic groups of interests, one of the colonies and the other of Great Britain, and the greatest problem facing men of the day was, as we see it now, that of reconciling the two. Would British statesmen prove themselves big enough to solve this problem of adjusting the colonial demand for greater freedom and independence to the equally imperative need of preserving the integrity of the empire, or would the differences go on widening and deepening until all hope of reconciliation was past and war only could decide the issue? We know the answer, for the War of the American Revolution shows the failure of the British policy, and proves also that the British ministries of the period after 1763, with their minds set on the value of the colonies from the point of view of profit, were wholly incapable of grasping that higher solution of the colonial problem, whereby these first self-governing dominions of Great Britain—the predecessors of Canada and Australia—might have been retained as part of the British empire. Evolution works as slowly in the world of ideas as in the physical world and it is not surprising that in the eighteenth century men did not conceive as a practical solution of the problem a union based on liberty and equality and cemented by ties of loyalty and affection. That was an idea which only another century of circumstance and experience, of a widening franchise and a growing democratic sympathy, could bring to birth in the British official mind. In the years before the Revolution the doctrine of mercantilism still acted as a barrier between Great Britain and her colonies.

Even so, the failure to solve the colonial problem in the way it has been solved to-day does not explain why

Background of the Revolution

reconciliation was not effected and some working form of adjustment arrived at. There can be no doubt but that at first the vast majority of the colonists did not want revolution. They looked on the connection with Great Britain as necessary and beneficial and preferred to maintain it as long as it was possible to do so. They would have been content with moderate concessions, and had such been made, it seems more than likely that the conservative majority in America would have been able to prevent the radical minority from going to extremes and committing the country to war. Over and over again, in studying the period from 1764 to 1774, we are driven to believe that a little more yielding, a little more of the spirit of friendliness and compromise, and a little less of British ignorance, stubbornness, and prejudice, would have calmed the troubled waters and stilled the storm that was brewing. Why a dispute about trade, which could have been ended with satisfaction to both parties, and a dispute about taxation, which in large part was quieted by the repeal of the acts that provoked it, should have been followed by defiance, coercion, and war, is one of the questions that cannot be answered except by a close examination of conditions not observable on the surface.

Such a study must concern, first of all, the mother country, an old, well settled, highly organized land, possessed of a mature national mind and a deep-rooted respect for history, law, tradition, and precedent, the best of whose people represented the high-bred, finely drawn product of a long social evolution; and, secondly, the colonies, new and sparsely settled and occupied by a frontier people instinct with individualism and possessed of but a rudimen-

General Reflections

tary sense of obligation and duty such as always accompanies membership in a loosely compacted social group. The people of Great Britain inhabited a small island which was insufficient for their needs, and if they were to grow beyond their narrow boundaries they were compelled to adopt "imperialism" and to become "citizens of the world." The colonists, on the other hand, inhabited the fringe of a vast, self-contained area of enormous potential resources, requiring concentration and intensive activity, conditions which tended to create a provincial rather than an imperial spirit.

Great Britain was at this time a long-established country, with the traditions behind her of more than a thousand years. These traditions were essentially feudal and aristocratic and persisted with amazing tenacity long after feudalism itself had passed away. In the eighteenth century there were no institutions, central or local, where aristocracy was not in control, and in probably no country of Europe was the law concerning land and hereditary property, the very buttresses of authority, justice, and social prestige, more feudal than in the England of that period. During the fifty years preceding the French Revolution of 1789, England was less like a democracy and more remote from the promise of a democracy than it had been under the Stuarts, for its law and policy were controlled by a very small number of men—landlords and money-lords—who, with all the limitations and prejudices of their order, saw but little beyond their own class interests and devoted their efforts to the maintenance of their own monopoly and the protection of their own social and political supremacy. For them alone was the world made. Law, education, religion, and even the colonies existed for their benefit. The lawyers gave support to their authority; the universities and public schools, degenerate and frankly materialistic, where cleverness seems to have been the conspicuous feature of academic life, catered to their prejudices and encouraged a conscienceless hunt for places and preferments; and the Church of England, whose rectors were often pluralists and non-residents and whose curates were generally underpaid and dependent, did not often trouble their souls with anxious and disturbing religious questions or threaten them with the wrath of an angry Creator. Men carried their theology lightly in that age of finished and unconscious cynicism, when scepticism had already begun to undermine the foundations of belief, and when literature, art, and learning, because they catered to the taste of a class and not of a nation, were rather dilettante than profound. The leading rule of life was to conduct oneself with dignity and composure, avoiding aggressive curiosity and passionate exuberance, and bearing oneself always with contentment and self-control. Men lived within the orbit of a narrow and conventional world, sanctioned by God and beyond the power of man to change and improve. Their social philosophy went no further than the acceptance of misery and vice as something inevitable and poverty as a condition for which God alone was responsible. The country gentry, the pillars of society and cornerstones of convention, worried but little about philanthropy and social betterment, because to alter the existing organization of society was an impertinent interference with the working of the divine will. To open the door of opportunity to the downtrodden and oppressed

General Reflections

masses would have been in their sight as great a contravention of God's purpose toward mankind as would have been the use of preventive methods to control birth or regulate disease. Each one, rich and poor, had his proper place in this social system and was expected to occupy that place with cheerfulness and resignation.

After the beginning of colonization in America, England passed through a long period of unrest, which ended in the so-called "glorious" Revolution of 1689, a turn of the wheel that secured new liberties to parliament and new powers to a group of governing families and a governing church but brought neither glory nor profit to the great majority of the English people. From this revolution England emerged into the placid waters of the eighteenth century, during which those in power firmly believed that their system of government was the best in the world and that to live under any other than that which England possessed was unthinkable. The era was marked by good feeling, except for the petty bickering of political factions, and by complacent satisfaction among those who held the reins of government. Heavy disabilities and penalties lay upon Roman Catholics, Unitarians, and Jews. Even Dissenters were barred from the borough offices, and of these only an occasional Dissenter had any share in legislation and the management of affairs. The members of the ruling caste were middle class in origin, representing the social element that had come to the front since the days of the Tudors. They were the rich *bourgeoisie* with reserves of capital to invest in various forms of profit-bearing enterprise. They were landowners and lords of manors, country gentlemen upon their estates, who legislated in behalf of the lands upon which they loved to live, and allowed their private interests to prevail over the welfare of the realm as a whole. This capitalistic aristocracy, which for many generations had supplanted the older aristocracy of the feudal type, controlled the voting, made the laws, and determined the policies of the government. Though not always agreeing with the rich merchants of the towns as to where should lie the burden of taxation, whether on land or commerce, they were in full accord with them in their eagerness for wealth; and while rarely decadent or depraved, they had an almost uncontrollable itch for money and were corrupt, selfish, and immoral. Perhaps never in the history of England had politicians spent so much of their time, energies, and abilities in the pursuit of riches as when the poor were living on the verge of starvation, when clerks in minor governmental offices could not get their legitimate pay, and when only here and there a man of small means could raise his head above the common herd and obtain any sort of political preferment. The activities of the ruling class were regulated by the only standards which they understood—birth, landed possessions, and money. Brains counted for little, and honesty, responsibility, and devotion to duty were more honored in the breach than in the observance. Bribery in elections, peculation and fraud in administration, avarice in family relations, and a general scramble for personal profit made the era one of sordid ambitions and an unjust distribution of wealth. England at the time of our Revolution was a middle-class hunting ground, in which civil and military offices were deemed legitimate prey for the spoiler.

Executive control lay in the hands of a Whig oligarchy,

General Reflections

and legislative power in parliament, which at this time was a kind of close corporation, screened from the outside world and secret in its proceedings, where the middle class reigned supreme. To publish debates or division lists was not only a high indignity but a notorious breach of privilege. The members, safe from publicity and, except in a few instances, independent of public opinion, were lax in attendance and dilatory in legislation, and were more concerned with the laws relating to middle-class interests than with such as provided for reform or laid down any great principles of government or administration. The welfare of those who had no votes was ignored and those who had no means of influencing a parliamentary election were rarely considered in the making of laws. The middle-class mind was not progressive. It was imbedded in tradition and dominated by fixed ideas of political and social relations. To this class alone belonged the right to rule; the poor had nothing to do but to obey. The rights of property were of more consequence than the claims of humanity, and human life seemed a great deal less important than the profits of capital. The idea of passing laws for the benefit and uplift of the lower classes—workmen, artisans, and agricultural and mining laborers, not yet awakened to class consciousness—was almost entirely absent from their thoughts. Their notion of the liberty won in the great and glorious revolution was liberty for themselves, not a general franchise for all the people, which in their minds would have transformed liberty into a plebeian tyranny. Even Burke could say that "our representation has been found perfectly adequate to all purposes for which a representation of the people can be desired or devised," and could boast further that the House of Lords was wholly and the House of Commons mainly composed for the defense of hereditary property.

The House of Commons, which originated the laws so obnoxious to the colonies, had become at this time the leading member of the lawmaking body, and the statutes, for the passing of which it was chiefly responsible, were beginning to supplant the executive orders in Council as instruments of government both in England and the colonies. This advance of the House of Commons to a position of leadership over the House of Lords, coupled with the control that both houses exercised over the crown, developed in the Commons a solidarity that hardly had existed before, and awakened in them a consciousness of power and authority, of independence and irresponsibility that rendered them extraordinarily sensitive to the liberties they had won. To "insult" crown and parliament as did John Wilkes in the *North Briton,* or to question their competency to legislate for America as did the radicals after 1765, was an act defiant of constituted authority, deserving condemnation and punishment. Members of the ministries and of parliament saw in the rioting and complaints of the colonials no manifestation of a legitimate discontent, but only disobedience and insubordination. As Secretary Conway, himself a friend of America, wrote to Governor Fitch of Connecticut, the king "cannot permit his own dignity and the authority of the British legislature to be trampled on by force and violence, in avowed contempt of all order, duty and decorum." Englishmen in office were beginning to believe that government by parliament, as it then existed, was part of the divine plan, and in so doing were exercising a prerogative as dangerous to the nation as was ever the divine right of the Stuart kings.

The official middle class was obsessed with a veneration of the constitution, a passion for legality, and a deep-seated hostility to reform, particularly of the crude and elementary franchise that made possible middle-class domination of political and parliamentary office. Although many among the lords of manors, who sat in parliament and made the laws of England, were capable of endurance and bravery and were gifted with the qualities of generosity and kindness, they were not, as a rule, well informed or open-minded men. They stood together like a wall and resisted appeals from any quarter that threatened to undermine the privileges of their class. Having won liberties for themselves, which they construed as inherent rights and not as concessions granted by grace or favor, they denied the liberties demanded by the colonists, and insisted that a British colony, by its very nature, was a subordinate and contributory part of the British system and must continue to be so as long as it remained a colony. Neither government officials, members of parliament, nor Englishmen in private life seem to have had any other solution of the colonial problem to offer than this of maintaining things as they were; nor could they have had one as long as they were obsessed by this idea of colonial subordination.

Among them were many who thoroughly disliked and protested against the government's policy of taxation and coercion of the colonies, and in 1775 some of the troops showed such an aversion to the service as to compel the ministry to consider the employment of foreign mercenaries; but it is doubtful if there were any, even among the best disposed of their class, including Pitt, Conway, Barré, Burke, Fox, and others friendly to America, who thought it possible to change in any important particular the policy that rendered the colonies profitable to Great Britain. Even Lord Effingham, who resigned his command rather than bear arms against America, objected only to depriving any part of the colonists of their liberties, "which form," as he expressed it, "the best security for their fidelity and obedience" to the king's government; and Adam Smith, though he considered some aspects of British policy toward America as "a manifest violation of the most sacred rights of mankind" and was disposed to favor complete separation, whereby "turbulent and fractious subjects" might be transformed into "faithful, affectionate and generous allies," still believed that it would be better to have no colonies at all than such as were unremunerative.

Such was England at the time of her trouble with the colonies: a land of two nations, one privileged, wealthy, and honored, divinely invested, as it were, with the right to rule; the other unprivileged, poor, and ignored, and according to the views of the time predestined by the eternal law to be ruled. The colonists faced an old country, with a highly developed and complex social organization, which was growing each year more and more industrialized, and in which manufactures, trade, and commerce—marks of a social and industrial state—were considered more important than agriculture; a country where the real conditions of an agricultural land like America were very imperfectly understood, and where rights based on history, law, and the possession of property were cultivated to the almost complete atrophy of those that were merely human.

General Reflections

They faced a dominant aristocracy, composed of less than one-fiftieth of the male population of the kingdom, sensitive, exclusive, and inclined to arrogance, deeply concerned for their land, business profits, and other vested interests, and caring but little for the finer spiritual aspects of art, literature, and religion. They faced a stubborn ruling minority, which exercised political power, monopolized the offices of state, dominated parliament, and indirectly determined the policies of ministries and shaped legislation to the advantage of their class. They faced a parliament, whose supremacy was unchallenged, for the nation as a whole had little control over its deliberations and was not recognized as exercising any appreciable influence on the conduct of affairs.

In contrast to this highly conventionalized social class, with its stereotyped, unprogressive system of thought and government, stood the American colonies forming in large part an agricultural frontier, with an environment that was favorable to the development of man as an individual rather than as a member of society. Frontiersmen have always awakened slowly to the importance of the communal interest. Distrustful of outside law and authority, suspicious of centralized government, and determined to enjoy entire liberty of action in domestic concerns, they have been wont to employ emergency methods, whenever convinced that in no other way could they obtain justice or secure relief. From Bacon's rebellion to the Regulators' War and from the activities of the Green Mountain Boys of Vermont, in opposing the authority of New York, to the vigilance committees of San Francisco in the early days

Background of the Revolution

of the American occupation of California, has the frontier exhibited a fearless and aggressive individualism.

Frontier settlers and pioneer communities, located far from the seats of organized authority, have developed their own ideas of government and have been accustomed to act upon the theory that the state was created by voluntary compact between contracting parties possessed of various inherent rights. This theory of the social compact has played a very important part in the history of American institutions, because of the constant presence of the frontier as the population moved westward, and has found itself expressed in various forms from the Mayflower Compact and the plantation covenants of the New England towns, through the agreements of the transient frontier states during the Revolution, to the schemes adopted by the local committees of Texas in 1835 and the vigilance committees of California in 1851 and 1856. Though before 1776 each of the British colonies in America had a well ordered and stable form of government of its own, that government (except in Connecticut and Rhode Island) was not of its own devising, and there was always existent an undercurrent of the frontier spirit—call it democratic if you will, though the word is not well chosen—which, though more or less dormant in the towns and the tidewater plantations, was insurgent in many parts of the back country and the mountain valleys, and omnipresent in New England, where (so all pervading was the habit of expressing opinions) it unconsciously determined political thought and shaped political action.

But not the whole of the colonial area was frontier in life and character. The older section along the coast was

General Reflections

made up of cities and towns in the North and of planta-tions in the South, where lived representatives of a wealthy and leisure class, commercially minded and conservatively inclined and given to oligarchic methods of government; while west of the "fall line" or head of navigation of the rivers flowing into the Atlantic a new frontier was in the making. Between the people of these two sections, as well as between the classes of the older region—the propertied and those without property, the conservatives and the radicals, the franchised and the unfranchised—there was beginning that time-honored and irrepressible conflict which was to play so prominent a part not only in the Revolution but also from that time to the present day in the history of the United States. However, during the colonial period, so predominantly was the whole area agricultural and so strong were the traditions of individualism already estab-lished that in contrast with the temperament of the mother country the prevailing spirit everywhere was that of the frontier. In all parts of this area, in varying degrees of in-tensity, the conviction existed that a people so far away from the ultimate source of authority had a right to con-trol their own political institutions. Our colonists cared less for efficient government than they did for self-govern-ment, and they paid less attention to the defense of their own borders and the preservation of law and order at home than they did to the securing of the right to govern themselves. Probably few if any among them realized the significance of their own promptings, and certain is it that no one in official England grasped the fact that the only way to save the colonies to the mother country was to grant them some measure of responsible government. The logic of historical processes is generally hidden even from the far-seeing men of any given age.

The territory of the new West, from the Lake Champlain to South Carolina—notably along the Susquehanna, in western Maryland, and in the Shenandoah Valley of Virginia—formed the frontier, properly so called, of the colonial area, and its occupants were too far removed from political and social contact with Great Britain to be much concerned with her affairs. It was in New England that the first cry of protest was raised against the policy of the mother country. There the towns—in most instances agricultural communities, dominated by the Congregational system of church organization—were accustomed to manage their own affairs. Glorying in their town and freemen's meetings, their ecclesiastical societies, their proprietary gatherings for the distribution and management of their lands, and the fact that they gave to every voting inhabitant an opportunity to take some part in the management of affairs, they were overcharged, as it were, with the spirit of self-government. Even their trainbands elected their minor officers, and placed in command men who sympathized with the radical, and often irresponsible, views of the rank and file. Connecticut, in particular, having always been free from interference by the crown and resident crown officials and having had fewer points of contact with Great Britain than had any of the other colonies, was filled with the spirit and practice of independency and held that the opinion of the individual was a fundamental factor in the life of a people.

Thus the environment of the New Englander produced an atmosphere of individualism that was congenial to the growth of the doctrine of natural rights independent of law, convention, and tradition, and was hostile to all ideas based on history, precedent, and man-made statute. These colonists fought with every species of difficulty that nature could place in their path—climate, stubbornness of the soil, amazing forests, and a stone-strewn earth—and they conquered nature because they were freemen, not slaves. Such an experience had its certain effect. "God and nature brought us into the world free men," said the Wallingford fathers, "and by solemn charter, compact, and agreement we came into the English constitution." Such a statement as this could not have been understood by a member of the British ministry or of parliament or by a legal adviser of the crown, and all of them would have called it meaningless, as from a constitutional point of view it was. They would have found similar views, uttered here and there in formal resolutions and private correspondence, not only unintelligible but positively dangerous and have dismissed them as merely the mouthings of theorists and radicals. Their attitude is well summed up in the remark of a contemporary Englishman, who in commenting on the preamble to the Declaration of Independence said that the American gentry assumed to themselves the inalienable right of talking nonsense.

It is not surprising that Englishmen found incomprehensible the language spoken in America, bristling as it was with ideas repugnant to the British governing class. Colonial grievances were real, but the arguments based upon them, drawn from the writings of Hooker, Selden, Sydney, and Locke, were often purely intellectual. In many of their resolutions and petitions the colonists pictured society as a political Utopia, unlike anything that ever had been in the history of the world, and far, very far, from that so-called "happy establishment" which Englishmen at home were at that time supposed to be enjoying. They spoke of liberty as if it were some inherent and inalienable right, possessed of men of all ages; and with amazing disregard of historical facts, they found in the past history of Greece and Rome and even of Great Britain herself ample precedents and illustrations upon which to base their contention. They believed that they had acquired these rights "as descendents of those who were parties to the Great Charter, and from those who possessed them, even before that happy era, under the Alfreds and Edwards of immortal name." All of which reminds one of the early claim of the New Englanders to their land as derived from God, "according to his Grand Charter to the sons of Adam and Noah."

The colonists did not seem to comprehend that "liberty" is in no sense a general right inherent in all men, but a vague word, entirely dependent for its value upon the sort of immunity it implies. The radicals in America were doing just what the feudal barons had done when they demanded "liberty" of King John; what the governing classes of England had done when they demanded "liberty" of the Stuarts; and what the people of England have four times done when they demanded and obtained "liberty" from parliament in the great franchise acts of the nineteenth and twentieth centuries. As organized and growing communities, they were demanding from king and parliament liberty to govern themselves in their own way, although in the exercise of their own sort of liberty

General Reflections

they themselves would deny political liberty to thousands among them, legal liberty to women, and personal liberty to slaves. They based their demand on the law of nature, which seemed to them an original law, grounded upon right, reason, and honesty, and beyond the power of the legislature to alter or diminish. This law they made the touchstone of their constitutional claims and, together with the habits of self-government and financial self-control which their own assemblies had formed, it warranted them in calling the acts of parliament "unconstitutional and illegal." Few of them based their claims on any closely reasoned argument or subtle analysis of the legal rights of the case; but acted rather from a subconscious sense of something wrong and unnatural in the British view of the colonial relationship.

The New England towns believed thoroughly in this most fundamental of all laws and continued so to believe long after they ceased to have any political connection with England. The Abington town meeting had this law in mind when it resolved that Boston's non-importation agreement of 1768 had "a natural and righteous tendency to frustrate the schemes of the enemies of the constitution and to render ineffectual the said unconstitutional and unrighteous acts." This is what the Sons of Liberty meant when, in the early days of their formation, they gave as one of the reasons for their existence "the preservation of the constitution"; and this it was that led Jared Sparks as late as 1832 to assert that King George in granting charters to the colonies had "assumed more power than the people approved." Whatever "the law of nature" may mean to us to-day, to the thoughtful colonist of that period it certainly meant justice, equity, and good conscience, or, as Hobbes puts it in the *Leviathan,* "every man's natural liberty to use his power to his own advantage." The colonists appealed to this law as to an ideal sense of justice, and on the strength of it they opposed the established rights of king and parliament. But opinions regarding a law of nature have undergone a change since that time. A natural right, which is a synonym for a law of nature, "has no existence," says a competent authority, "save in its potential exercise; does not proceed from within but is permitted from without, and is a phrase empty of other meaning than to denote whatever primitive or acquired inclinations of man each individual is by common consent allowed to realize. These permissions have varied and will vary with the ages—no argument based upon the dogmatic premise of natural rights can reach anywhere save in drifting fog." If this be true, then our forefathers, profoundly convinced though they were of the fundamental soundness of their own convictions, which had to be expressed in a very high key to drown troublesome discords in the lower notes, were able to justify their revolt by an appeal to an hypothetical political philosophy. Yet despite this assertion and despite the thirteenth, fourteenth, and fifteenth amendments and the statue in New York harbor, Americans are very far from being agreed to-day on the subject of liberty and the natural law.

There is no doubt that the more intellectual among the colonists honestly believed in the existence of these original and inherent rights of all mankind and in the sacredness and inviolability of the "liberty" that they claimed for themselves; but their forcible demands, couched in the

General Reflections

form of resolutions, petitions, declarations, and addresses, and characterized by many varieties of phrase and degrees of temper, were merely attempts to obtain for an act of revolution the support of eternal verities. Early in the movement, they would have been satisfied with a reasonable amount of responsible government granted by crown or parliament and a measure of recognition, at least, of the position attained by their own assemblies; but as time went on and no concessions were made until after their alliance with France in 1778 they repudiated all offers of peace and obtained complete legal independence by force of arms. Had Great Britain conceded even a portion of the independence enjoyed by her self-governing dominions to-day there would have been no American Revolution. The colonists were not contending for democracy, popular government, or universal suffrage. They had what they wanted of these things, for to the extent that their popular assemblies were responsible to their communities while parliament was responsible to no one, they enjoyed at that time even a greater measure of popular self-government than had the British nation itself. The War of Independence was not fought to make even America safe for democracy. With independence won democracy would come in America's own good time, just as it would have come had the colonies remained attached to Great Britain. In either case the time would have been deferred for many years, for a property qualification on the right to vote lingered long in this democratic country of ours. Until very recently it applied to the election of city councils in the state of Rhode Island.

We may, if we like, call the British authorities unimaginative and insular in failing to see that the only way to relieve the colonial discontent was to yield in some measure to the demands of the colonies. The accusation is not without warrant, for the ministerial leaders of Great Britain were statesmen of second-rate abilities, without knowledge and without vision; but there is reason to think that in 1770-1773 even far-sighted statesmen would have failed to understand the issue involved. In common with all conservatives of the time the men in office looked on the colonial agitators as dangerous radicals. Middle-class Englishmen, who had no difficulty in appreciating grievances about trade and grievances about taxation—for both were tangible and concerned what they knew best, money—could make little of these constitutional claims of the colonists or their talk of the law of nature and of nations, of reason and of God. They knew of the law of nature, but rather, as Sir Frederick Pollock has said, "as an appanage of polite society than as a constituent of technical jurisprudence," and Blackstone made use of it at second or third hand "to ornament—but only to ornament—the introductory chapters of his *Commentaries*." To apply the law of nature, as the colonists were doing, to such a practical matter as the sovereign power of parliament was to threaten that "beautiful form of civil government" from which they derived their influence and under the protection of which they were secured in their offices and possessions. They realized that the claims of the colonists, if recognized, would undermine the foundations of the existing political order, and ranked as seditious anything, whether in England or America, which endangered the integrity of the British constitution or threatened to impair in any important particular the

General Reflections

value of the colonies as an asset to the mother country. Against this immutable dictum of the ruling classes the unprivileged masses of Great Britain hurled themselves in vain for fifty years; but their fellow agitators in America, further advanced than they in political education and three thousand miles away, were in no mood to accept as decisive such an unyielding mass of conservatism and prejudice and won their complete independence in a single act of revolt.

The final break came because the British authorities had but one remedy for radicalism, either in England or America, and that was coercion. The age was not one of conciliation or compromise. However much Burke may have pleaded for a greater measure of freedom for America and Pitt may have wished to substitute a policy of friendliness and affection for one of brute force, the majority in parliament was not favorable to concession. The landowning gentry, who were lords of manors, justices of the peace, and autocrats of the counties in which they lived, viewed restlessness and discontent not as manifestations of genuine distress that ought to be relieved, but as evidences of sinful depravity and congenital ingratitude toward the best of kings and the wisest of ministries. Grenville said in the House of Commons that the protests of radicals, both in England and the colonies, were infamous libels, which tended to stir up sedition and rebellion and could not be passed over with impunity. The government believed that uprisings should be suppressed by force, outrages visited with fine and imprisonment, offenses against those in authority dealt with as acts of insubordination, public meetings forbidden as menaces to peace and order, and radical speakers and writers treated as demagogues and malcontents. They held that disobedience was contumacy, opposition defiance, and hostile criticism (to quote from the indictment of John Horne, 1775) "false, wicked, malicious, scandalous, and seditious libel, of and concerning His Majesty's Government." Such was the spirit of the ruling classes in England in the eighteenth century. That men in authority were influenced by it for twenty years after the century had closed, the Gag Laws of 1819 attest; and that similar methods of governmental control have not been unknown elsewhere since the days of the Revolution, the American Alien and Sedition Laws of 1798, the German *Ausnahme Gesetze* of 1878, and sundry occurrences of more recent date in this country bear ample evidence.

Such obstinate adherence to the divine right of established authority was met on the American side by charges of oppression and tyranny expressed in terms of extreme bitterness and reproach. The radical leaders would tolerate no "doctrine of passive obedience or any other doctrine tending to quiet the minds of the people in a tame submission to unjust legislation and control." Should Great Britain succeed in her policy then, they contended, would "they and their posterity be enslaved as deep as any Spaniard or African"; with liberty expiring, they would become "veritable Israelites in bondage, deprived of happiness and even of life itself." Everywhere there sprang up local organizations with appropriate symbols—Sons and Daughters of Liberty, with their Liberty Trees and Ensigns of Liberty—whose duty it was to resist to the utmost the "inexorable enemies of American freedom." At first these bodies were not revolutionary or even radical in member-

General Reflections

ship, but were composed very often of men and women of all grades of opinion who desired no change of government or of relationship with Great Britain. Later, however, they lost their moderate character, and their members, finding that words were of slight avail, resorted to deeds of violence. They not only defied the acts of parliament but, convinced that their own colonial governments had failed them and were impotent to meet the necessities of a critical situation, carried their idea of "liberty" to its logical extreme, and derided both the authority of their own courts and the laws of their own assemblies. These muscular radicals, like their fellows in every revolutionary movement, became a law and authority unto themselves, construed the "law of nature" as a "law of license," and giving themselves free rein inflicted injuries, destroyed property, and even threatened the lives of those who resisted or opposed them. Such conduct was a true manifestation of the emergency spirit of the frontier, under the stimulus of which men banded together in various committees of safety, intelligence, and correspondence, county conventions, and provincial congresses. These bodies, unauthorized by statute or charter but generally managed with order and decorum, were called into being for the punishment of unpopular and undesirable persons and the pursuit of revolutionary ends.

Familiar as this spirit is now to the student of American history, it was not familiar to the contemporary Englishman across the sea. If to the colonists the British government seemed oppressive and tyrannous, to the ruling class in England the colonists seemed dangerous and rebellious, and addicted to opinions and practices that were subversive of the most cherished tenets of their political faith. British political philosophy had no place among its precepts for the doctrines that were stirring the souls of the colonists, and contemporary British thought was as yet untouched by the dynamic principle of evolution. We must not forget that the British ruling class, as well as the colonial radical leaders, had a philosophy of government, and that in the answers which exist to the Declaration of Independence, they gave voice to some of its tenets. As expressing the British point of view, these answers and other similar writings are illuminating, but they show an utter failure on the part of most Englishmen of the period to comprehend the significance of the movement in America. However, these men could hardly have been expected to appreciate the fact that the colonies in cutting loose from their mother country were but obeying a law of general evolution of human society toward higher and broader forms of government and social relations.

In searching for the minor causes of the American Revolution, one should consider, first, the royal governors. Some of these men, such as Martin of North Carolina, seemed wholly unable to realize that the royal system of government was breaking down, while others, such as Bernard of Massachusetts, though knowing that the royal executive had already become powerless in the face of the local discontent, could see nothing but anarchy in the movements taking place about them. Secondly, one should pay more attention to the privy councilors and departmental officials in England, who comprehended even less than the governors the failure of the British administration in the colonies and the need of vital changes if royal authority were to be in any measure restored. And, finally, one should lay far more stress than is usually done upon the influences of the legal advisers of the crown and departments, who, in their opinions rendered in parliament, on the bench, and in written reports, adhered with the utmost strictness to the letter of the law. The legal mind of the eighteenth century, amazingly defiant of the teachings of history and equally forgetful of the claims of justice and humanity, treasured tradition, precedent, and technical devices, but rarely, if ever, groped for the reason lurking beneath acts defiant of established authority. It paid little or no attention to law as a social institution and probably would have denied vehemently, had the point been called to its attention, that a rule of law ought to justify itself by the way it functions under existing social and economic conditions. In the days of our Revolution no stress was laid in England on the economic and social utilities that to-day are recognized as underlying rules of law. Even as late as 1840, the crown lawyers were still adhering to the old view of the status of a colony. Their attitude during the years preceding the reform act of 1867 led Bulwer-Lytton to say that the lawyer in England looked and looked diligently into English law, established by custom, precedent, or act of parliament, and knew all the nice points and proud formalities on which legal justice rested and by which it might be evaded, but they viewed the study of legal history and legal principles as worse than useless. Even as late as 1875, we are told that many British barristers had "a way of looking at the law, not as a system intended to bring about the best justice possible and to be developed for that purpose, but merely as a bundle of traditions with no concern for their existence other than that they are what they are." Lawyers of this literalist type, or, as they have been called, of the Procrustean school, were very loyal to authority, within which they stood (says a recent writer) "as within a fortification. If you tell such an one that the letter killeth but the spirit giveth life, he asks you for the reference, and then when you give it, he says that he has not got the book in his library."

In examining the part that the lawyers played in bringing on the Revolution, we find ourselves placing well known names under indictment, the names, for example, of Thurlow, Wedderburn, Mansfield, and Blackstone, the most conspicuous legal lights of their day. Thurlow and Wedderburn, respectively attorney general and solicitor general, answering Dartmouth's query regarding the character of the proceedings of the first Continental Congress, declared that "the seising the public money and new-officering and disciplining the militia, for the purpose avowed and insisted upon, in the resolutions of the provincial congress, amount to high treason, and the several resolutions, ordering the same, are overt acts, by which to prove the same, and the being present at a meeting, where such resolutions were taken, is prima facie evidence of the crime of treason." This opinion was delivered on February 2, 1775, nearly four months after the "Declaration" of the first Continental Congress was adopted, and must have served to encourage those already bent on a policy of coercion. Mansfield never wavered in his adherence to that policy, and on the subject of the power of parliament said "that the British legislature, as to the power of making laws, represents the whole British empire, and has authority to bind every part and every subject without the least distinction, whether such subjects have the right to vote or whether the law binds places within the realm or without." Blackstone by his famous treatise confirmed the ruling classes of England in their overweening conceit of power and flattered them by expressing entire content with the law and constitution of England, as they then existed. He was an opponent of every suggested reform and, as a critic puts it, "toadied to the sinister interests and mischievous prejudices of the party in control." He represented what Jefferson has finely called "the honeyed Mansfieldism of Blackstone," which "turned the old lawyers from Whigs into Tories."

It seems to have been true of the lawyers of the eighteenth century in England (and we cannot say that it has not been true of some of them since that time, even in our own country) that however strong and warm might be their sense of justice in ordinary matters, their minds automatically closed when the legal aspects of a case came up for consideration. Men thus constituted were not fitted to pass judgment upon the claims and grievances arising in America. The hostility of the frontier for the lawyer, from early colonial times, through the Regulators' War, Shays's Rebellion, and the Whiskey Rebellion, to the days of far western settlement, is well known and needs no elaboration here. It is crudely illustrated by the homely remark of a frontiersman of later date, who on being jailed for manslaughter protested indignantly against the outrage in the following vigorous terms: "Now-a-days you can't put an inch or so of knife into a fellow, or lam him over the head with a stick of wood, but every little lackey must poke his nose in, and law, law, law is the word. Then after the witnesses swear to their pack o' lies, and the lawyers get their jaw in, that old cuss that sets up there high and grinds out the law to 'em, he must have his how-de-do. I tell you I wont stay in no such a country. I mean to go to Texas, where a man can have some peace and not be interfered with in his private concerns."

It is true that in fixing the responsibility for the Revolution we must attribute much to the obstinacy, prejudice, and personal government of George III, to the unfriendliness, stubbornness, and duplicity of Hillsborough, and to the subservience and good nature of Lord North; but more important than the personal influence of any of these was the inability of British officials and lawyers to depart in any essential particular from the strict interpretation of the law and the constitution. They would permit no encroachment upon the royal prerogative or denial of its powers; they would allow no reflection upon the authority of parliament or protest against its acts on the ground of unconstitutionality; and they would admit no change in their mercantilist policy or alteration of their time-honored method of managing the colonies in the interest of trade and commerce. The official and legal mind of England was dangerously near that state of immobility which courts either degeneration or revolution, petrifaction or destruction.

It is a more difficult matter to decide whether or not George III deserves the sentence of execration to all eternity that has been passed upon him by nine-tenths of the American people. In our Declaration of Independence he is made responsible for many things with which he had nothing to do, and for nearly a century and a half has been the scapegoat of the Revolution. But the fact is that the influence of George III was not the same at all stages of the revolutionary movement. It played but a small part in the period before 1774, when the king was merely one of that stiff-necked body of Englishmen who made up the ruling classes, holding opinions and prejudices that were characteristic of his order and identifying himself heart and soul with the system against which the colonists revolted. He could pray as devoutly as anyone else of his kind that the British constitution might remain (as he himself expressed it) "unimpaired to the latest posterity as a proof of the wisdom of the nation and its knowledge of the superior blessings" it enjoyed; and, even after the war was over, he could say that the age was one "when disobedience to law and authority" was "as prevalent as a thirst after changes in the best of all political institutions" and that in order to stem these evils it required a degree of temper and sagacity such as was to be expected only "from a collection of the best and most calm heads and hearts" that the kingdom possessed. After 1774, however, his influence became more direct and personal and he must share equally with his ministers and the members of parliament whatever guilt belongs to a group of political leaders who could see but one course to pursue and that a course characteristic of the age in which they lived. George III was a thorough believer in coercion as the only remedy for insolence, and both he and his ministers were upheld in that belief by a majority of the English electorate. After 1778 the situation changed again and George III fills the scene as the one outstanding figure to whose stubborn persistence and almost criminal obstinacy was due in largest part the prolongation for five long years of a burdensome and costly war. More and more of those who had given him support saw both the hopelessness and the unwisdom of the struggle; the ministerial majorities in parliament dwindled; the friends of America increased in numbers; demands for the cessation of the war became more insistent and attacks on the crown more frequent; and both North, his own chief minister, and Barrington, his secretary at war, warned him of the ruin that might follow the continuance of so disastrous a purpose. Yet the king held on, yielding only to the inevitable after the cause was lost, and consenting very ungraciously to a change of ministry and the beginning of negotiations for peace.

There can be little doubt but that many of the impressions which we have formed of George III and of his place in the history of our Revolution are due to his later and not his earlier conduct. We read the words of his letter to the Corporation and Livery of the City of London in 1775, as if they were sufficient to fasten upon him for all time responsibility for our revolt. In fact, however, they were but the embodiment of the opinions of his ministers and other British officials, of the majority in parliament, and, as far as we can judge, of the greater part of the ruling class in England at that time. We do not like the sound of those words: "It is with the utmost astonishment that I find any of my subjects capable of encouraging the rebellious disposition which unhappily exists in some of my colonies in America. Having entire confidence in the wisdom of my Parliament, the Great Council of the Nation, I will steadily pursue those measures which they have rec-

General Reflections

ommended for the support of the constitutional rights of Great Britain and the protection of the commercial interests of my kingdoms," but they merely echoed the sentiments of the extremists in England, who at this juncture were in the governmental saddle. Davies, in his treatise, *The Influence of George III on the Development of the Constitution,* says truly that George III "was one of the most popular kings that ever lived with the average elector —with the middle classes and the Tory squires. As a general rule his opinions and his prejudices were those of the average elector, and frequently they afford a good index to the public opinion of the time—so far as that can be estimated." As to the king's views on the quarrel with the American colonies, Davies adds, "the prejudices of the King were the prejudices of his people."

If we are to consider the king as in any way responsible for the original estrangement of the colonies from the mother country, it must not be because of his personal influence but because of his constitutional position as the embodiment of the royal prerogative—a power upheld by such lawyers as Blackstone and wielded rather by the king's councilors, secretaries, and executive departments than by the king himself. The royal prerogative in its application to America was disliked and opposed by the colonists as a power exercised by someone outside themselves and hence conflicting with their management of their own affairs. Yet it was authorized by the law and custom of the British constitution, as part of the common law, and those who were responsible for its use would brook no encroachment upon it. As far as the colonists were concerned, it is doubtful if George III ever attempted to assert the power of the prerogative more than had William III or Anne or even his own immediate predecessors, and it is a curious fact that except for a few paragraphs concerning special events of the period, due to the adoption of the coercive policy, there is not one of the major charges contained in the Declaration of Independence that might not have been brought against any of the sovereigns of England from 1689 to 1760, as justly as against George III. But in fifty years times had changed and the colonists had changed with them, and in 1775 they were no longer willing to endure what they had borne for many years without serious protest. In revolting against the prerogative, the colonists were opposing a legal convention of the constitution rather than a man, and the Declaration, though directed against the king as a "tyrant" and as one "unfitted to be the ruler of a free people," was in fact an indictment of the constitutional power of the prerogative. It was not, because, truthfully, it could not be, an indictment of a man, whether of German descent or otherwise.

When some years after the close of the Revolution a strong Federalist reaction took place against it, and President Dwight of Yale, "Pope" Dwight as he was called, could say that it had "unhinged the principles, the morality, and the religion of the country more than could have been done by a peace of forty years," opinions of George III underwent a modification in certain quarters. There was a disposition to look more kindly upon him by those Americans who knew somewhat of his personality, and Professor Benjamin Silliman, who had traveled abroad in 1805 and 1806, could speak of certain sentiments of the king as "characteristic of a magnanimous and superior man, and as certain to go far toward invalidating unfavorable popular impressions" of him. But later incidents revived the bitter memories of the "unnatural war waged by a wicked ministry against this country," as a contemporary called the attempts of the British government to suppress the colonial revolt; and in the years that followed George III gradually acquired a rare collection of vices, the choicest of which, perhaps, were added during our own Great War, when he was charged with having been responsible for the American Revolution because he was to all intents and purposes a German king, or, as it was expressed by one writer whose patriotic zeal outran his knowledge, a Prussian king. Such ignorance leads one to conclude that inasmuch as popular impressions are never scientifically accurate and in history are notoriously unreliable and as the historical knowledge of a good many persons consists of an enthusiastic belief in a few things that are not so, it is often true that in matters of historical judgment the *vox populi* resembles the voice of the devil rather than the voice of God. Sometimes in exasperation at the perversities of politicians, legislators, school boards, public orators, newspaper writers, and even librarians, who represent the Fundamentalist mind in the field of history, one is tempted to enlarge upon Carlyle's well known remark about majorities, and to conclude that truth is the voice of one crying in the wilderness and public opinion the voice of those who cry "Crucify Him." On the question of popular judgment in arts and letters, Ruskin was right in pointing out the illogic of expecting the opinions of a crowd to be correct, when the opinions of any individual in that crowd were more than likely to be wrong. So in the matter of historical opinion it is difficult to believe in the divinity of the masses and to accept the view that just because they are numerous they must be right.

The American Revolution, like nearly all revolutions in history, was an uprising not against a king and his ministers, but against a system and a state of mind. Nor was the system the work of George III, Hillsborough, Townshend, or Lord North, for they were its products not its creators. It was the result of the Revolution of 1689, which gave power to the men of the landowning and monied classes of England. They, although they bore titles of nobility and constituted the county aristocracy, were of middle-class origin and under their rule were fashioned those rigid and sinister ideas of power and government which permeated the whole official world of king, ministries, parliament, council, departments, and boards, all having to do with administration at home and abroad. The governing classes of England were face to face with a problem such as never before had confronted English statesmen, and the nature of which they did not recognize or understand. They did not see that just as an original stock transplanted to a new soil perpetuates the best qualities of the old but develops faster than the mother plant, so the colonies in America were far more advanced, politically, socially, and morally, than the mother country and could not longer be held in leading strings. Having diagnosed the case wrongly, they applied the wrong remedy, that of coercion, which not only did not cement more closely the colonial relationship but destroyed it altogether. The problem was not one of mercantile subordination or of imperial authority, but concerned the very constitution of the Brit-

General Reflections

ish empire; and such constitutional concessions as would have satisfied the demands of the colonists, these British statesmen could not make, because they were barred by the mental limitations of their own time and class. Only the threatened collapse of the entire colonial system in the thirties of the next century, the rise of a group of young enthusiasts who refused to believe that matured dependencies were necessarily foreordained to revolt, and a ten years' war with the stubborn bureaucracy of Downing Street finally convinced the British official mind that colonies might be entrusted with responsible self-government and still be retained as parts of the empire. Though we find—and rightly—much to criticise and much to blame in what the older statesmen did and did not do, we cannot in all justice hold them responsible for not foreseeing and adopting a policy that emerged, under new conditions and after many humiliating experiences, three-quarters of a century later. To do so would be to blame all governments of the present day for a tenacious adherence to policies that may be completely reversed during the next fifty or a hundred years.

In this brief inquiry I have made no attempt to discover with any idea of finality the causes of the American Revolution. I have done no more than present a point of view and suggest certain lines of investigation that might be followed in an effort to understand that momentous event. The historian cannot with dignity and self-respect allow the field to be preëmpted by the propagandist, the hero-worshiper, or the patriotic partisan. The subject is too weighty, its significance too great, and its place in the his-

Background of the Revolution

tory of human progress too vital for it to become merely the handmaid of controversy or the fetich of a misdirected national patriotism. In dealing with it we cannot afford to neglect those wider aspects which connect our history with that of the world at large. We owe it to ourselves, as one of the great nations of the earth, to study our colonial and Revolutionary periods, not as isolated and provincial phenomena, but as phases of a great forward movement, worthy of that creative analysis which the scientist gives to the operations of nature and the scholar gives to other movements that have played their parts in the evolution of the human race. In approaching these subjects with enthusiasm and courage, a wider range of knowledge and sympathy, and a greater detachment from modern prepossessions, the historian will honor his people and do justice to himself, and the history that he writes will lose none of its distinction because it endeavors to embody the truth. A nation's attitude toward its own history is like a window into its own soul and the men and women of such a nation cannot be expected to meet the great obligations of the present if they refuse to exhibit honesty, charity, openmindedness, and a free and growing intelligence toward the past that has made them what they are.